READ, WRITE, & SPELL

A Complete Language Guide for Home Education
Preschool–Grade 3

READ, WRITE,

&

SPELL

A Complete Language Guide for Home Education
Preschool–Grade 3

TALITA PAOLINI

Paolini International LLC
Livingston, Montana USA

Published by Paolini International LLC
P. O. Box 343
Livingston, MT 59047
U.S.A.

Visit us online: paolinimethod.com

Manufactured in the United States of America
First Edition

**Publisher's Cataloging-In-Publication Data
(Prepared by The Donohue Group, Inc.)**

Names: Paolini, Talita.
Title: Read, write, & spell : a complete language guide for home education : Preschool - grade 3 / Talita Paolini.
Other Titles: Read, write, and spell
Description: First edition. | Livingston, Montana : Paolini International LLC, [2019] | "Paolini Method, learning by doing"--Cover.
Identifiers: ISBN 9780966621358
Subjects: English language--Writing--Study and teaching--Activity programs. | Reading--Study and teaching--Activity programs. | English language--Orthography and spelling--Study and teaching--Activity programs. | Education, Preschool--Activity programs. | Education, Primary--Activity programs. | Creative activities and seatwork. | Home schooling.
Classification: LCC LB1576 .P36 2018 | DDC 372.62--dc23

Cover design by Tara Mayberry: TeaberryCreative.com
Author photo by Immanuela Meijer

CONTENTS

WELCOME

My husband, Kenneth, and I educated our two children, Christopher and Angela, at home. What began as a hands-on endeavor blossomed into a story that amazes even us. Homeschooling gave our son and daughter the freedom to develop their personalities without peer pressure, the opportunity to pursue projects that intrigued them, and the time to play, dream, and exercise. Now adults, our children are grateful for a childhood environment that allowed them to explore their interests and nourished their innate love of learning.

From the time Christopher and Angela were infants, we spent lots of time talking and reading with them. Numbers and letters became familiar through games, art projects, and daily use. Our nature observations led to animated discussions about how things work, followed by experiments to see what happened. We listened to music from classical, folk, and contemporary composers; learned about people who lived in other times and places; and read about distant lands. Although this was before easy access to information through the internet, our children learned that whatever their interest, they could find library books to satisfy their curiosity and expand their understanding of the world.

When Christopher was ready for first grade, we were living in Anchorage, Alaska. Kenneth and I discussed the situation and realized that although our son was only six, he was doing third grade work. He would be out of place emotionally and physically in a classroom of eight year olds, although academically he was working far beyond a first grade curriculum. We knew the state of Alaska provided distance learning programs for students who lived in isolated areas and thought perhaps we could access those materials. But when we spoke with school officials, we were informed that our son would be required to take a battery of psychological tests before they would exempt him from the regular public school system. Believing that submitting Christopher to those tests was unnecessary, we decided to continue homeschooling.

I had trained as a Montessori teacher with a remarkable lady, Dr. Elisabeth Caspari, who had the privilege of working directly with Maria Montessori, creator of the Montessori Method. From Dr. Caspari, I learned the principles of early childhood education: how children think and how they learn. Later, to meet the needs of my own children, I adapted these classroom techniques and developed new lessons, tailoring projects to use everyday household items and fit the home environment. Each activity was created to meet specific developmental and educational goals.

Late at night before falling asleep, I reviewed the day and our children's behavior. What motivated their actions? What caused the rough spots? What fascinated them? Then I would think of lessons that tapped into each child's interest, trying to match the information each one needed to learn or skills they needed to practice—reading, writing, math, etc.—with activities that sparked their innate curiosity and engaged their attention. Angela loved stickers and cats, so many projects included those. Including movement was especially important for Christopher. For both children, hands-on elements—building, cooking, gardening, collecting, sorting, counting, drawing, or painting—made the educational process more fulfilling and enjoyable.

Kenneth inspired our children to stay physically fit and mentally sharp with daily exercise. He shared his wit, critical thinking skills, money management expertise, and a healthy dose of skepticism in a scam-filled world. In addition, his love of books and maps kept a supply of new reading material flowing into our home.

We felt it was important that our children get accredited high school diplomas to facilitate their college applications, so they took correspondence courses through American School. Working at an accelerated pace, by choice, Christopher received his diploma shortly after his fifteenth birthday. Angela—not to be outdone—received hers *before* her fifteenth.

Today Christopher is listed in the Guinness World Records as the youngest author of a bestselling book series, the Inheritance Cycle. Angela is the author of several screenplays.

A Book Is Born

So why this book? Over the years when parents asked us for homeschooling advice, my husband and I invited them into our home to learn about our projects and teaching strategies. Notebooks filled, they departed with a renewed sense of direction for their endeavors. I also spoke with parents of public and private school students who were looking for ways to supplement their children's classroom experience. All recommended that I write a book so more people could benefit from what we had learned. I liked the idea, especially because I wanted to document our method for Christopher and Angela to use with their future children.

After several attempts to organize the information, I decided to focus on language first, and this book was born. Kenneth, the computer whiz in the family, helped format it for publication.

Read, Write, and Spell is designed to give you a wealth of activities to enrich your child's learning experience and help you teach with confidence. The lessons progress sequentially, from preschool through early elementary. Many of the illustrations and examples are taken from actual projects our family made. We used these activities to raise happy, intelligent, well-educated, in-love-with-learning young people. We hope that you find them useful as well!

Getting Started

Babies begin acquiring language skills from the day they are born by hearing and watching people talk. After a year or so, they begin to form words and gradually link them into sentences. Reading and writing—more abstract ways of communicating—are acquired later. Children as young as three and four can learn the sounds of letters and begin to read and write simple words. From that point, it just takes practice to become proficient.

Teaching your child the fundamentals of language is really quite simple. The first step is to associate the letters with their sounds. It is easy to then arrange the letters into words. From that point, he makes the mental leap to understand that words represent real things and ideas, which allows him to read with comprehension. Meanwhile he learns how to write. All this is covered in Part 1 and 2 of *Read, Write, & Spell.*

Part 3 introduces letter partners, combinations of two or more letters—such as *th* in *thank, ai* in *rain,* and *ph* in *phone*—that make sounds that are different from their individual letters. Your child becomes familiar with these by writing them in booklets. Activities later in this manual provide lots of practice with these new words.

When your child is comfortable reading and writing, turn to Parts 4–6, where you'll find lessons that help him practice spelling, expand his vocabulary, compose paragraphs, write in cursive, create reports, write for fun, and use basic grammar and punctuation.

Although this book contains numerous activities, don't feel that you must do them all. The collection of projects is the result of taking a large course of study and dividing it into small steps. The lessons near the beginning are appropriate for children ages three and up.

If your child is just starting to read and write, work straight through the manual. If he is more advanced, look through the following list to find his next learning goal, then start there. The number(s) to the right of each goal indicates its corresponding lesson. The **bold** numbers highlight the most important projects in each group, ones that teach key concepts. Nonbold numbers mark lessons that provide additional practice, enrichment, or new information of lesser importance.

Part 1—Prereading and Beginning Writing
These activities show you how to teach your child the fundamentals of language:

- Develop vocabulary and observation, listening, and speaking skills: 1

- Match objects and pictures: 2, 3

- Associate pictures with words: 5

- Recognize and say the sounds of the letters: **4,** 6, 7, **8,** 9

- Strengthen fingers in preparation for writing: 10, 11, **12**

- Write the letters: **13,** 14

- Associate written words with objects: 15

- Blend letter sounds. Beginning reading: **16, 17**

- Recognize capital and small letters: 18, 19

- Write his name: 20

- Matching words and pictures. Beginning reading: 20

Part 2—Short-Vowel Words: Beginning Reading and Writing
The second set of lessons works with short vowel words—phonetic words like *cat, hen, spin, frost,* and *nut*—and covers these topics:

- Read and write short vowel words: **22,** 23, 24, 25

- Read and write short vowel phrases: 26

- Read and write smaller letters: **27, 32**

- Use helping words (non-phonetic words needed to read and write simple sentences): **28**

- Recognize and use the period, question mark, and exclamation point: **29**
- Read and write short vowel sentences: **29,** 30, 31, 33, 34, 37
- Chart reading progress: 35
- Make a book of color names: 36

Part 3—Partner Words

This section introduces partner words—such as *rain, mule, thin, ship, light,* and *ghost*—that contain two or more letters that say a different sound together than they do separately. The lessons help your child develop these skills:

- Expand vocabulary and improve spelling by reading and writing booklets of partner words: **39, 40,** 41, 42, **45, 46, 47**
- Read partner word sentences: 43, 44, 48, 51, 52, 53, 54, 55
- Write number words: **49**
- Follow the days, weeks, and months on a calendar: 50
- Recognize more non-phonetic helping words: **38, 51**
- Write sentences using partner words and use commas properly: 53

Part 4—Activities to Build Vocabulary

With these projects, your child continues to improve his reading and writing skills while expanding his vocabulary:

- Build vocabulary with games and projects: 56, 57, 58, 59
- Read new words and increase his reading speed, with comprehension: 60, 61, 62
- Write in cursive: **63**
- Write a paragraph: 64
- Write short stories and notes: 65, 66, 67
- Spell new words in a Spelling Notebook: **68,** 69, 70
- Understand and use contractions: 71

Part 5—Creative Reading and Writing Projects

Once your child has learned the basics of reading and writing, use these activities to develop more complex language skills:

- Write descriptive paragraphs and short stories: 73, 76, 77, 78, 79, 80, 81, 82, 84, 85

- Read for content: 72

- Learn how to write a letter: **74,** 75

- Write poetry: 86

- Make a joke and recipe book: 83, 87

- Create a favorite subject guidebook: 88

- Build vocabulary with a crossword puzzle game and dictionary race: 89, 90

- Correspond with an imaginary pen pal: 91

Part 6—Learning More About Language

The book concludes with more advanced lessons that prepare your child to explore new topics with confidence:

- Write a book report: 92

- Form a book club with friends: 93

- Write a report on a place: 94

- Write a biography: 95

- Learn the basics of grammar—with rainbow colors and games: **96, 97,** 98, 99, 100, 101, 102

- Learn about antonyms and homophones—with a hands-on project: 103

- Create a personal journal: **104**

Once you understand the Paolini Method of presenting lessons in steps, making books, and building projects around your child's interests, you can easily apply the concepts to other subjects.

How to Make Your Home
Learning Friendly

We lived in several places when our children were young, including a rustic log cabin that leaked through holes in the caulking when it rained. Yet wherever we were, we created a space—even if just a corner—dedicated to learning.

Take a few moments to think about life from your child's point of view. Squat down and look at your home from her level. What do you notice? Are things clean, accessible, inviting? Does she have a place to put her things? With these observations in mind, take steps to improve her environment and give her a quiet, comfortable area to focus on projects.

What To Do:

- Try to give your child a spot of her own, with a child-sized chair and table or desk. Make sure the space has plenty of light, keep the surroundings clean, and decorate with a pretty picture or a plant. Inform family members that her things should not be touched without her permission, and that she should not be disturbed when working. Multiple children can share a workspace as long as each has her own section.

- Provide paper, pencils, ruler, tape, glue, scissors, etc., arranged in one or more decorated cans or baskets.

- Eliminate noise distractions, such as people talking, telephones, televisions, radios, or other sources. If this is impossible, some children find that wearing headphones and listening to quiet music can isolate them from the surrounding chaos enough to let them concentrate.

- Some children work well with quiet or cheerful background music; others are distracted. Let your child's response guide your decision on whether or not to provide it.

- Minimize clutter. Have a designated place to store school materials. Explain that these are not toys; they should be treated with care and put away immediately after each use. Emphasize that everything has a "home"—a basket or box or shelf—and that when she is finished using an item, she should return it to its home.

- Three great additions to the schoolroom are a bulletin board, a calendar, and maps:

  - Make a simple bulletin board by putting clear contact paper over a piece of poster board and mounting it on a wall. The contact paper allows you to tape and remove items from the board without ripping its surface. Use the bulletin board to make seasonal or monthly displays, show pictures and charts from study units, and highlight your child's most recent art or writing. It makes a great centerpiece for a homeschool work area, reflecting the current curriculum.

  - Having a wall calendar makes it convenient to mark off the days. This helps your child understand the passage of time. At the beginning of each new month, discuss and note upcoming special events, such as birthdays, holidays, outings, and new study units.

  - Hang maps of your state, country, and the world on a wall. Help your child find locations on them when world events are mentioned in the news, letters or e-mails are received from distant friends, or places are mentioned in reading material. Ask her to name states, countries, or oceans bordering each location she finds and point out any outstanding geographical features, such as lakes, rivers, or mountains.

Make a Home Library

Since the internet allows instant access to information, why have any books at all? Too much screen time is not good for developing brains, and many people find that they retain information better when they read it in a physical book, rather than from an ebook. Perhaps that is because the experience is multi-sensory: as you turn the pages, each volume reveals its own feel, smell, and look. Curling up in a cozy reading nook with a real book will help your child develop a love a reading.

Keep an abundance of books and magazines in your home to cultivate a family reading habit. Children imitate the adults around them, so if you read, they will want to do the same. Create a mini-library for your child. In addition to story books, build a collection that includes a dictionary, thesaurus, and reference works on subjects that interest her, such as flowers, dinosaurs, trains, butterflies, rocks, or horses. The next time she needs to identify something, she will have the resource at hand, and during her search, she will probably encounter other fascinating things.

What To Do:

- To make your child's personal library, get a small bookcase—or a couple of cardboard fruit boxes covered with patterned contact paper—and place it in her room, school area, or other "special place" where reading materials are safely stored when not in use. Stock it with her favorites, as well as with reference and library books. Add to it regularly. Include a rectangular basket to hold the booklets she makes from the lessons in this manual.

- Help her expand her home library. If your local public library has a yearly clearance sale, pick up some items at bargain prices. You can also find deals in the youth sections of used bookstores.

- Surprise your child with books throughout the year. Let friends and relatives know that books or magazine subscriptions are appreciated as gifts.

Create an Inviting Reading Area

Place a pile of cushions or a bean bag or other comfortable chair on a little rug next to her home library. Provide a lamp for adequate light. A favorite stuffed animal or two will enhance the friendly atmosphere.

A Final Thought

You are part of your child's learning environment. Remember that your presence is more important and influential than any lesson you assign. She watches and imitates your actions, your attitudes, your responses to events. And she forms opinions of herself based on your comments about her. You and the people who surround her are her role models, so do your best to set a good example for her to emulate.

Conversation

Infants first hear the sound of their mother's voice in the womb. Following birth, they become aware of their surroundings, soaking in the speech sounds that are the building blocks of language. If you observe a baby's expressions, you can catch a glimpse of his experience as his brain brings order to a deluge of sensory input.

During the first two years of life, babies listen intently to conversation, which helps them understand and speak their native tongue. Three year olds commonly know over a thousand words. That number will triple or quadruple over the next year. Preschool children delight in learning new words, asking questions, and participating in conversations. Their ability to narrate a sequence of events or follow a set of directions grows year by year.

As a child's vocabulary increases, so does his ability to organize his thoughts and express himself clearly. Here are a few ways to help your child develop his conversational skills.

What To Do:
- Talk to your child from birth. Help him learn to speak by explaining what is happening around him. Say, for example, "Oh look! The rabbit is nibbling on the lettuce."

- Say words clearly. Speak slowly and face him when introducing new words, so he can see how your lips form them. Research has shown that baby talk helps infants focus attention when they are learning the building blocks of language, but once that foundation is established, use proper grammar to set a good example for him to emulate.

- When your child begins talking, ask him to describe what he experiences and thinks about. Engage him in discussions on many subjects. Use complete sentences and encourage him to do the same.

- Urge him to express his thoughts, feelings, and needs clearly, with respect and empathy for others.

- Teach him, by your example, how to respond politely to others. Insist that he use appropriate language. Discourage him from using slang or swearing.

- Recite poems and rhymes. Sing songs together.

- Introduce new words into your conversations to increase his vocabulary and show him how to replace imprecise words with more descriptive ones. Encourage him to tell you new words he learns and to ask you the meanings of those he doesn't understand.

- Outings are great ways to expand your child's vocabulary and teach him about the world. When possible, bring him along when you shop or do errands. Explore interesting places such as parks, playgrounds, museums, bookstores, and historical sites. Find a time when customers are few, then stop by a small bakery, art gallery, cheese factory, chocolate shop, yarn store, florist shop, or other small business and ask the shop keeper to describe his or her specialty. After the visits, discuss your adventure.

- Record your child singing, telling a story, or reciting a poem. Hearing himself talk may help him speak more clearly.

- Celebrate his playful experiments with language. Building vocabulary and learning how to pronounce and use words properly takes years; enjoy the path he takes on that journey toward proficiency.

Example:
Games, rhymes, poems, and word play help your child become more familiar with our rich language. Correct him when he mispronounces words: don't encourage him continue saying *pascetti* (spaghetti) just because it's cute; instead, teach him how to say the word correctly. If, however, he enjoys the way *pascetti* rolls off the tongue, then set it in a silly rhyme with the real word:

> Pascetti, pascetti
> I wonder if it's ready?
> Spaghetti for you,
> Spaghetti for me.
> Spaghetti! Spaghetti! Spaghetti!

Cultivate Listening Skills

By listening to your child with your full attention, you pave the way for thoughtful communication in the years to come. Ask him questions, get his opinions on various issues, then offer your views and explain why you hold them. His ideas may be different from yours, but value his honesty in sharing. Through discussion, he will learn that you respect his thoughts and feelings and that he can express his viewpoints without fear. Likewise, encourage him to listen attentively when others speak. Doing this will help him develop empathy for others, along with tolerance for diverse points of view. Although, as the adult, you make the final decisions on things, try to tailor your choices with his perspective in mind.

READING

Reading helps your child learn about people and the world, experience wonderful adventures, and educate herself about many topics. While this book explains how to decode words, creating a good reader requires more. A nurturing environment where reading is part of the daily routine enjoyed by adults as well as children is important.

Give your child many opportunities to practice reading. Assist her early efforts with a series of handmade booklets that progress from one-word to one-sentence to a short paragraph on each page.

Once she is familiar with simple words, she is ready to read books from the children's section of your local library. If you are unsure where to start, ask a librarian for recommendations. Encourage your child to review the books often to strengthen her confidence and sense of accomplishment. Then gradually introduce longer ones with words of increasing complexity. As her skills improve, she will start choosing her own books and reading for pleasure.

What To Do:

- Begin reading to your child when she is still a baby, cuddling her on your lap and holding the book for both of you to see. Describe the pictures, trace your fingers under the words as you read, and sometimes guess what might happen next. Show her how to turn pages gently and treat books carefully. Make reading a pleasant experience so she associates it with happy feelings.

- Encourage family members to read together.

- As she learns the letters and then words, bring her attention to them on signs, food labels, and magazines. Praise her for discovering them in her environment.

- Read to toddlers and preschoolers daily. Although it can be annoying to adults, it is normal for them to ask you to read the same book repeatedly.

When a story is finished, review what the characters experienced and how that made your child feel. Ask if she agrees with their choices and actions.

- Once she is able, have her read to you. Congratulate her on her new skills. For variety, take turns reading sentences and paragraphs.

- Make sure the reading area is well lit. Headlamps or clip-on book lights are handy when other lighting is insufficient.

- Continue reading to your child even after she can read for herself. Hearing stories from books that are beyond her own ability expands her vocabulary and encourages her to try harder material.

- Make a habit of reading books, magazines, and newspapers yourself each day. Keep them handy in the bathroom, by the bed, and near a comfortable chair. Even if you read most things electronically, try to have some physical materials around. Establish a quiet time in the evening when family members read before sleep. When your child sees you reading daily and discussing the interesting things you learn, she will naturally want to participate in the family activity.

- Visit bookstores together and browse through volumes on subjects such as arts and crafts, science, stories, animals, cooking, or whatever strikes her fancy. Let her buy new discoveries as rewards for work well done. Give her books as gifts. And don't forget used bookstores, which offer lower prices and will often buy or give credit for your used books.

Visit Your Public Library Often

Your local library holds a treasure trove of stories, along with fascinating books on diverse topics. Introduce your child to the youth librarian and ask for reading recommendations. Locate the sections holding biographies; through these you can meet famous people like Alexander Graham Bell, Helen Keller, Anna Pavlova, the Wright brothers, Clara Barton, and George Washington Carver. The science section is full of illustrated books explaining the basics of science, how our bodies work, and all about the exciting world of animals. Locate the geography and history sections, with their volumes waiting to transport your child to faraway places or distant times. Read folk tales from cultures around the world. View works of great artists. Together, spark your creativity with books filled with art projects and holiday craft ideas. There is so much to discover in the library, if you take the time to explore.

Invite your child to get her own library card and make visiting the library a weekly or biweekly event. When she shows special interest in a topic, have her borrow books on the subject to learn more. Ask if your library hosts children's programs. If they have a newsletter, get on the mailing list so you can attend events.

Take Care of Library Books

Teach your child to make sure her hands are clean before holding a book and that books must never lay scattered on the floor. They should be treated with respect and kept on a designated shelf or in a specified box or bag. Have her mark a calendar with the due date and return the books on time.

The Internet

The internet is a wonderful resource where you can find information and videos on any topic and get support from experts. In addition, it provides a way for your child to interact with the larger world, with sites that link her with a pen pal in a distant country, help her learn a new language, or work through math problems at her own pace. But it comes with dangers, as an innocent search can lead to perilous territory. Find sites that are safe for youngsters to explore, and limit accessibility with child safety software. The internet is certainly the place to go for a quick answer when your child asks why the sky is blue. Just keep in mind that it provides a different experience than browing through stacks of books, their covers enticing her to peek inside. Both are great ways to learn about the world.

But Mom, I Hate to Read!

When our son, Christopher, was learning to read, he found sounding out words frustrating. "I hate to read!" he told us emphatically. Every day we encouraged him to practice a little and add stickers to his reading chart. He persevered, motivated by our promise that adventure stories awaited him.

One day, during one of our weekly trips to the library, he found a series of children's mystery stories that fired his imagination. That was the turning point. Thereafter he read with enthusiasm and pleaded for more books.

Since then, he has read thousands of books and now values them as much for what they can teach him as for the stories themselves. Learning to read broadened his understanding of the world. History, science, art, adventure, science fiction, fantasy, biographies, and classics all helped him explore our amazing earth, along with the ideas and dreams of diverse people. Perhaps Christopher's words, written years ago as a child, express it best:

Books
On a long forgotten shelf,
Through dust and grime,
Hidden treasure you will find.

A golden vessel to carry you far,
Through raging battles and riding saddles,
Through fairy glens and hidden fens,
Through darkened plain and mourning pain,
Through dragons lair and pirate's flair.

Over mountains and tumbling fountains,
Over kingdom castles strong and fair,
Through dungeons dark and grey . . .

But when you close the book,
POOF! it goes away.

WRITING

The ability to write well enables students to express their ideas clearly and logically. Learning to write is a step-by-step process. First, children become aware that letters are associated with sounds and that words have meaning. Later, they practice forming those letters and words themselves. A young child's scribbles help him build finger strength, thereby improving muscular control in preparation for writing. Once the basics are learned, it becomes more a mental exercise as students learn to organize their thoughts into sentences and paragraphs.

What To Do:

- Bring a young child's attention to written words by pointing out—and having him point out—places where text is used: advertisements, magazines, books, e-mails, letters, game instructions, recipes, cereal boxes, maps, etc.

- Encourage young children to scribble, draw, and color.

- Before your child is writing, jot down little stories and poems that he dictates. Let him decorate the pages, then form them into booklets.

- Provide a desk and chair that are stable and promote good posture. Ideally, your child's feet are supported by the floor, the writing surface is a few inches below elbow height, and the chair allows him to sit upright without slouching.

- Encourage good posture when writing. If you notice that he is often hunched close to his work, it is possible that he needs corrective lenses, so have his eyes examined by a professional.

- Demonstrate how to hold a pencil with a relaxed grip. Observe his form over time to be sure he doesn't clench his fingers. Also, encourage him to write with movements that originate more from the wrist than the fingers. Practicing good habits as he learns to write keeps tension in the hand and arm at a minimum, thus eliminating stress.

- Provide many opportunities for your child to practice writing. Be patient and don't expect perfection; he will improve over time!

Examples:
- Create a shopping list together (an older child can do this himself). Have him cross off each item as you find it at the store.

- Write him notes and have him respond with his own.

- Encourage him to write thank you cards for gifts he receives and to acknowledge the thoughtful acts of others.

- Ask distant friends and relatives to send him letters or postcards. Encourage him to write back.

- Find out what your child cares about—what fires his imagination—and have him write about those things in small projects or in a journal. Let him know that he is free to express his thoughts and feelings on paper without your censure. Many budding writers are discouraged by criticism and stop trying. A friendly word or smile may encourage your child to persist, whereas a disapproving comment may end his efforts.

In short, provide opportunities for your child to write each day and let him write about things that interest him. Praise him for his efforts and keep it fun!

MAKING BOOKS

A key element of the Paolini Method is making and reading little books. These fall into two categories: those you make for your child and those she makes herself.

1. Books You Make

What To Do:
- To make picture books for pre-readers, glue images on a few sheets of paper or cardstock. Staple the pages together or punch holes down one side and tie them together with yarn. Beginning books can be simple expressions of your life and surroundings.

Example:
Before our second child was born, I made our one-and-a-half-year-old son, Christopher, a *Baby Book*. The pages were 5- by 6-inch cardstock; the writing was with blue marker. I cut out pictures from a catalog and glued them on the left pages, printing the name of each item underneath. On the right pages, I wrote sentences that described the items. Christopher "read" the book over and over with me in preparation for the coming of his sister, Angela.

- Cover: The Baby Book (decorated with small marker-drawn flowers)

- Picture of a smiling baby: Hi! I am a baby.

- Picture of a bottle: This is my bottle.

- Picture of a rubber bottle nipple: And here is the nipple from my bottle.

- Picture of a highchair: When I get bigger, I will sit in a highchair to eat.

- Picture of a baby ball: This is my ball. It is blue, yellow, pink, white, and red.

- Picture of a car seat: I sit in a car seat when I ride in the car.

- Picture of a baby with diaper: Look! Here is my diaper.

- Picture of a blanket: This is my blanket. It keeps me warm while I sleep.

- Picture of a crib: This is my crib. I sleep with my blanket in the crib.

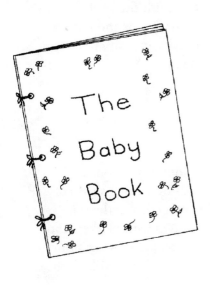

- Create books for older students with words, sentences, or paragraphs on each page. Ten pages is a nice length. As before, punch holes down one side and bind the pages with yarn. No special literary talent is needed to create unique books that your child will treasure.

- Collect your child's work in language, math, science, geography, history, and art into books. Seeing that you value her efforts enough to form the loose sheets into a booklet will encourage her to do her best. Every time ten pages or a study unit is completed, add a construction paper cover, write on a title and the date, and secure the pages by stapling at the side or punching holes and tying with yarn. Knowing that ten pages concludes a unit offers her incentive to do a little extra work to "finish the book." This gives her a product of her own she can proudly read to friends and relatives, thereby reviewing the material. Older students can take an active role in reviewing their schoolwork and binding it into books.

2. Books Your Child Makes

What To Do:

- Once your pre-reader is familiar with library and homemade books, show her how to create ones of her own. Make pages by cutting sheets of construction paper into quarters and stapling them together at the side. Invite her to fashion her book by "writing" on the pages with markers and crayons, decorating them with stickers, or by gluing on pictures cut from magazines, catalogs, or downloaded from the internet. When finished, she can proudly "read" the book to family and friends.

- An older student may use half or full sheets of paper for her books. She can draw illustrations or glue in pictures related to her topic, then write words, sentences, or paragraphs to complete the project.

Tips for Teaching at Home

It is normal for children to show interest in learning to read and write at different times. To facilitate language development, encourage conversation by asking questions, discussing events, and sharing your observations; read to your child often; and provide him with writing materials. Let his attention level guide the pace of your instruction. Whether you homeschool full time or coach your child after school, these ideas will help you be an effective teacher.

- Be your child's cheerleader! Praise him not only for his accomplishments but for work that may seem clumsy but is a fine attempt at a new subject or demonstrates progress on a project. (Note that you are complimenting him for his efforts, not for sloppy or thoughtless work.) Acknowledge his endeavors to improve when he tries new things, stays with a task just a little bit longer, or works a bit faster.

- Relax! Try not to be too critical of his efforts. Remember that learning is a process and that his skills will improve with practice. If you observe him making mistakes in a certain area, don't criticize what he just did but present the material in a lesson *later* to help him improve.

- Be patient. Some days will be better than others; sometimes he will work at a slower-than-average pace, sometimes faster. Don't be concerned by small setbacks but know that as long as he is progressing, all is well.

- Create projects based on subjects that interest him. Compelling him to do work that he hates or pushing him to try things he is not ready for will only make him feel frustrated. So try to find activities that engage his attention while improving his skills. If, for example, he loves horses, encourage him to read about them, then include them when writing poems and stories. In addition, he could draw a picture of a horse and label the parts, make a booklet listing one breed per page, or label a map with their places of origin. If one topic bores him, suggest he try another. The most important thing is that he reads and writes daily. Your job is to give him every opportunity to practice these skills and praise him for his efforts.

- Allow him to express his creativity by giving him the opportunity to experiment, to try things for himself. He will remember the results of those little adventures far better than if he were just told the probable results and never experienced them.

- Keep in mind that your child's attention span may vary, depending on his mood, health, and events in his life. One day he may focus on an activity for thirty minutes, another day five, so pace the lessons according to his level of interest.

Having Problems?

Trust your instincts. You hear all kinds of rules for parenting and teaching from well-intentioned people. Listen to what they have to say, then use what makes sense. Above all, trust what your child is telling you, both verbally and through his actions and attitudes. If he is unhappy or "causing trouble," try to find the root of the problem by watching his behavior and thinking about what it means:

- Does he need more time with you?

- Does he need more interaction with people or less?

- Is he too busy? Is a too-full schedule making him feel stressed, irritable, or unable to meet other people's expectations? Does he need time to just play, daydream, and think?

- Is he getting enough exercise? Make sure that he has time to run, jump, and stretch multiple times daily.

- How is his sleep schedule? Is he getting ample rest or is he tired?

- Is he eating a nourishing diet? Make sure he gets protein at every meal, along with fresh fruits and vegetables. Limit sugary foods and drinks.

- Does he want to learn about a specific subject but has no time or resources to do so?

- Is he testing the limits of your authority?

- Does he have daily goals that are attainable?

Your child is a person, just like you, although his brain is still maturing. Try to understand his point of view, then identify actions you can take to address his behavior challenges. If you need help, ask people you trust or professional coun-selors for advice. Above all, try to make decisions based on what you think is best for his development. Sometimes a superficial solution will obscure the symptom of a deeper problem that should be addressed through a more thoughtful, although perhaps not so convenient, approach.

A Lifestyle of Learning

- Establish a rhythm of daily activities. In the morning, for example, go to the calendar, sing a song, give your child a hug, and talk about the day's plans. Reconnect with him after work sessions with an embrace, a snack, a song, a walk, or a lively dance to help ease tension and "get the jiggles out." End the day with more hugs and kisses. Put aside any discord and tell him that no matter what, you will always love and care for him.

- Make reading part of your family's lifestyle and limit electronic pastimes. Keep fun, interesting books and magazines available; add new ones from bookstores or the library often. Give him quiet time to listen to great music, read books, observe nature, and think.

- Supervise what your child watches on TV, the music he listens to, the computer games he plays, and the company he keeps. He will absorb much of what he reads, sees, and hears, so try to make it the best.

- Set rules for important things—like being kind to people and animals, treating objects carefully, telling the truth, and obeying a direct order. Enforce these firmly. But within these rules, allow him broad freedom to experiment. Sometimes he will make mistakes or create a mess; other times his project will be a success. In each case, what is key is the *process* of trial and error that leads to discovery, not necessarily the result.

- Don't sweat the little things. When the inevitable misfortunes of life happen—your child breaks a glass or spills a drink, for example—keep the incident in perspective. We've all had accidents, no big deal, but your response to the situation will show him how to cope with these events. Anger accomplishes nothing in the way of repairing the damage, so take the opportunity to model a calm solution to the problem. Look at the mess with him, discuss what happened—explaining that you are sad at the loss—and then engage his help to clean it up. Talk about what he can do in the future to avoid making the same mistake.

1, 2, 3, . . . Mini Steps Make It Easy!

Divide large lessons into engaging small units so students can tackle one portion at a time. For example, instead of asking a child to learn all the alphabet letters at once, present a new one each day. Approaching projects in this manner will help youngsters develop a habit of working enthusiastically toward goals they can achieve. A series of little victories builds their confidence, and the happiness they feel at completing each project makes them eager to do another.

Jonathan's Story

Jonathan, a nine-year-old boy, was fascinated by ancient Egypt—pyramids, mummies, and so forth—so his mom helped him find library books and websites on the subject. He was delighted! But when she announced that he would be required to write an essay on it, his enthusiasm faded; the joy went out of his research. What began as a project of self-motivated discovery became clouded by the dread of writing a boring report and getting nagged by his mom to complete it.

Imagine instead that each morning a new mini-project was presented that included an activity and a bit of writing. On Monday, for example, he would draw an outline map of Egypt, sketching the Nile River with blue pencil and adding little brown triangles for pyramids. He could then write a sentence, such as, "The Nile River is the longest river on Earth," to accompany the map. The next day he would build a pyramid from sugar cubes and again write a sentence or paragraph about the monumental structures. He could compose a story about a mouse watching the construction of the pyramids, make a "papyrus" scroll, find out about the work of scribes and try his hand at making hieroglyphs, jot down a few interesting details about a pharaoh of his choice, make a timeline of pharaohs, study how the Nile River affected the agriculture of the region—and then draw pictures of the native crops and foods—investigate mummies, etc. When he was ready to move on to another subject, these pages could have been formed into a book. Jonathan would then have had a beautiful report filled with interesting pictures and descriptions about the subject that fascinated him—and he would have done it with pleasure, one step at a time.

Supplies:

What You Need

The following items are used in lessons throughout the book. Most can be found at an office supply, stationery, or discount store. Brightly colored markers, pencils, and paper—along with cheery stickers and pictures—lend activities an element of fun.

Lead Pencils: Younger children may be more comfortable working with a larger diameter pencil, but many find a regular No. 2 pencil satisfactory. If you can find them, get a few softer-lead pencils. They produce a thick line, which is nice for beginning writers.

Soft-lead Colored Pencils: Writing with beautiful colors is more enjoyable than working with a lead pencil. To help your child distinguish the vowels *(a, e, i, o, u)* from the consonants, he writes them with different colors: vowels in blue, consonants in red. Other lessons ask for additional colors. I recommend you purchase a few high-quality, soft-core colored pencils (such as Prismacolor) for these lessons, because they lay down a thick line of vibrant color with minimal pressure. You can find these sold as "art pencils" at art and stationery stores.

I don't recommend using the colored pencils sold in packs at the grocery store for the lessons, as they are made from harder material, which means they require more pressure and produce a thin, pale line.

Crayons: Crayons are wonderful for scribbling, coloring, and decorating. Although they are not called for often in this book, they—along with watercolor and tempera paints—are important for your child's art exploration.

Stickers: Useful as incentives and for marking finished work on charts, stickers can also inspire stories and be incorporated into creative writing projects. Many children enjoy using them to decorate completed work.

Pictures: Collect magazines and catalogs with interesting pictures: cars, food, clothing, plants, animals, people, toys, foods, tools, etc. You can also print out images from the internet. These are useful to illustrate booklets for young children. Older students can incorporate the pictures into books of their own.

> **Downloadable Pictures:** For your convenience, I have created outline art to accompany some of the lessons in this book: www.paolinimethod.com/downloads
>
> - Alphabet Pictures, large
>
> - Alphabet Pictures, small
>
> - Short Vowel Word Pictures, large
>
> - Short Vowel Word Pictures, small
>
> - Partner Word Pictures

Plain Paper: Sold in packages as copy, printer, or multipurpose paper, it is used to make pages for books and other projects.

Lined Writing Paper: Several sizes are used. Beginning writers work on large paper (child's ⅞-inch-rule writing paper), then graduate to small paper (⅝-inch-rule) in Lesson 32, Writing Smaller. Purchase pads of these in stores or download my free printable templates. Older children can write on wide-rule or college-rule notebook paper.

> **Downloadable Writing Paper:** www.paolinimethod.com/downloads
>
> - Large paper: ⅞-inch-rule lined writing paper
>
> - Small paper: ⅝-inch-rule lined writing paper

Construction Paper: Slightly thicker and larger (9 x 12 inches) than printer paper, construction paper usually comes in multicolored packs. It is essential for making book covers and other projects.

Cardstock: This paper, stiffer than plain paper but not as thick as cardboard, is great for making booklets for very young children.

Poster Board: Found at discount or art stores, these large, stiff sheets of paper are great for mounting on the wall and are used to make bulletin boards and calendars.

Glue: Plain white glue works well for the projects in this book.

Scissors: Purchase good quality scissors that cut well, with little force. Give young children rounded-tip, child-safe ones.

Ruler: A simple wooden or plastic one-foot ruler is fine. Choose one that is cut straight on the end, for accurate measuring.

Yarn: Homemade books are often bound with yarn. Vary the color for variety. Colored string or thick cotton crochet thread also works well.

1-Hole Punch: Available in discount stores, this tool is handy for punching pages that are then bound with yarn into books.

Stapler: Sometimes all you need are a few staples to bind a booklet.

Dictionary: Whether online or physical, a dictionary is an important resource for improving vocabulary and checking spelling and word meaning. I also recommend having a thesaurus.

PART 1

PRE-READING &

BEGINNING WRITING

Perfect for preschool and kindergarten children, the activities in Part 1 begin with games that help youngsters improve their ability to identify, name, and match items; relate spoken words to pictures of corresponding objects; and expand their vocabulary.

The lessons later in this unit show you how to introduce the letters' basic sounds and how to blend them. Doing these activities gives your child a strong foundation in phonics and leads to that exciting moment when he makes the connection between an object in the real world and the letters before him—the moment when he reads his first word!

This section also contains projects to strengthen the fingers in preparation for writing. Your child first learns to draw lines, curves, and circles, then puts those shapes together to make letters. With a bit of practice, he will write his name and simple words with ease.

Throughout this unit, you gather your child's completed pages into booklets for his home library. Repetition is an important part of learning, so encourage him to review these books often.

Let's get started!

❧ 1 ❧

NAMING OBJECTS AND PICTURES

These simple activities set the foundation for future language work. Identifying and discussing different items helps your child develop his vocabulary and learn more about the world.

☞ What You Need:

Set of objects or pictures in one subject that captures your child's interest, such as animals, cars, toys, colors, fruit, or shoes; basket or box

☆ Activity 1: Naming Objects

As you and your child go about your day, slowly and clearly say the names of objects both inside your home and out. Use every opportunity to expand his vocabulary by talking about what he sees. Sit with him and look at collections of things or pictures. Name the items, have him repeat their names, then discuss your observations.

☆ Activity 2: Three-Part Naming Game

This three-step activity is done over days or weeks, according to the readiness of your child.

Step 1: This Is . . .

Set out three to six objects or pictures in a horizontal line. Say the name of each item as you set it down. Invite your child hold each item and say its name. To conclude the activity, hand him each item while repeating its name, and ask him to put it away in a box or basket. Encourage him to say the item's name one final time as he puts it away.

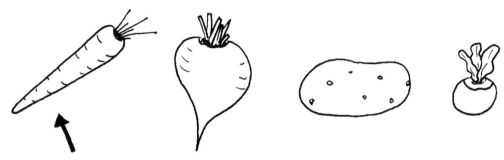

This is a carrot.

Step 2: Point to the . . .

Set out three to six objects or pictures in a horizontal line. Say the name of an item and ask him to point to it. Mix the items. Name a different item and ask him to point to it or hand it to you. Vary this by asking him to carry the items and place them "on the chair, on the table, under the table, by the plant," etc., and then one by one bring them back. The aim of the exercise is to have him recognize the name of and correctly select each item.

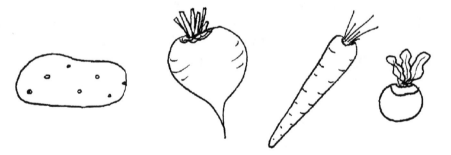

Can you point to the radish?

Step 3: What is This?

After lots of practice with Steps 1 and 2, set out objects or pictures as before. This time, point to an item and ask him to tell you its name. Say, "Jason, what is this?" When he can answer easily, he has mastered this activity.

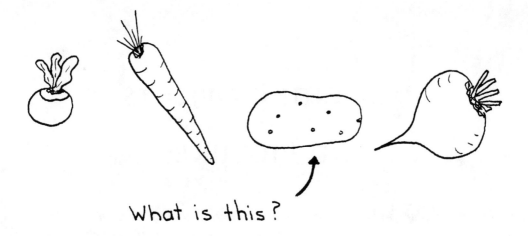

Note:

These steps—called the Three Period Lesson, by Dr. Maria Montessori—are a great way to introduce new concepts in language and other subjects. They can be used to teach big, medium, small; triangle, square, circle; cold, warm, hot; and any number of other things.

If your child says an incorrect name in Step 3, observe where he needs more work, smile, and then put the project away. Another day, return to Steps 1 and 2 and present the lesson again. Be patient; repetition is an important part of learning.

Your role is not to criticize or correct but to help your child learn for himself, to facilitate mastery through practice. Adults often want to rush to the final step—to push the child to give the right answers when time would be better spent reinforcing the names in Step 2—but only when you are sure he can correctly identify the items should you proceed to Step 3. Remember that every time he is successful, he builds confidence, which feeds his enthusiasm to learn more.

⁓ 2 ⁓

MATCHING OBJECTS

AND PICTURES

In this activity your child will match objects to objects (such as two bananas), objects to pictures (such as a shoe with an image of one), and pictures to pictures (such as matching identical famous paintings). Doing this helps her develop visual discrimination and understand that a picture represents a real thing.

☞ **What You Need:**

Objects to match, pictures, cardstock, scissors, glue

✂ **To Prepare: Picture Cards**

Cut blank cards from cardstock and either draw or glue on sets of matching pictures in categories such as vegetables, frogs, clothing, houses, people, nuts, etc. Postcards of places or things also work well for this.

☆ **Activity 1: Matching Objects to Objects**

1. Place one set of objects in a neat vertical row on a table or rug. Place the second set of objects randomly to the right.

2. Take an object from the random set and place it next to the item it matches. Do this slowly and deliberately. Look at the object you will match and consider where to place it. By doing this, you show your child to look, think, and decide before matching. Either match all the items the first time while she watches—and then let her have a turn by herself—or match one or two items and let her continue.

Example:
Try matching these objects:

- Fruit: apples, oranges, bananas, lemons, grapes

- Vegetables: carrots, potatoes, celery, tomatoes, cucumbers

- Tools: hammers, screwdrivers, wrenches, flashlights, trowels

- Silverware: forks, knives, soup spoons, teaspoons, serving spoons

- Socks: match by color or style

- Shoes

- Colored soaps

- Leaves: match by color or shape

- Rubber insects

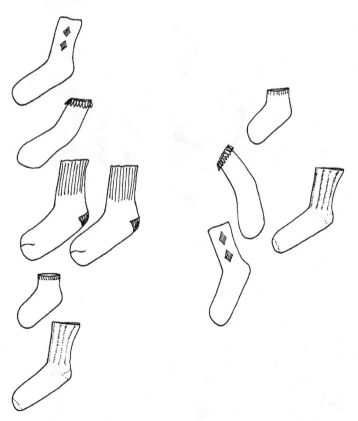

☆ **Activity 2: Matching Objects to Pictures**

1. Place one set of Picture Cards in a horizontal line. Place a matching set of objects at random below.

2. Pick up one object and examine it carefully. Look at the Picture Cards in turn, and then place the object beneath the card it matches.

3. Repeat with the remaining cards. Invite your child to repeat the exercise with this or another set of objects and cards.

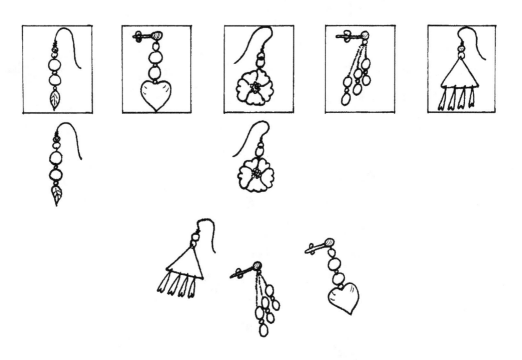

☆ **Activity 3: Matching Pictures to Pictures**

1. Place one set of Picture Cards in a vertical line. Set the second set of Picture Cards to the right, at random.

2. Pick one of the random Picture Cards. Look at it intently and then look at the line of pictures to find the one that matches. Place the Picture Card next to its mate.

3. Repeat with the remaining cards. Invite your child to repeat the exercise with this or another set of Picture Cards.

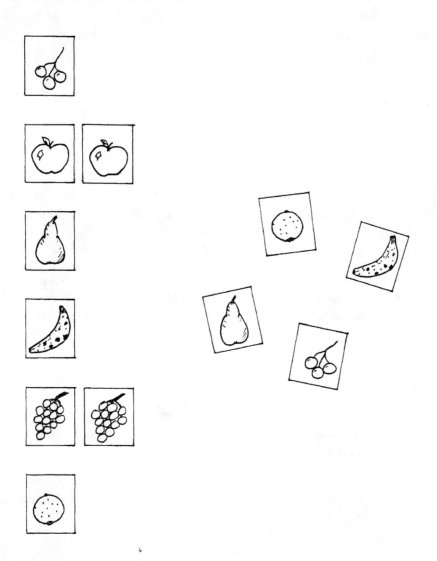

❧ 3 ❧

PICTURE MATCHING GAME

This variation on a traditional game is easy to make and helps your child develop his observation and memory skills. Although it is usually played with two or more people, some children enjoy playing it alone.

☞ What You Need:

Cardstock, ruler, pencil, scissors, matching pictures, glue

✂ To Prepare:

Decide how big you want to make the game. For young children, start with twenty cards. Older children enjoy games of up to one hundred cards.

1. Cut cardstock into 2½- by 3-inch rectangles.

2. Draw or glue sets of matching pictures onto the cards. Choose pictures of things your child enjoys, such as birds, toys, pretty holiday items, dinosaurs, or airplanes.

☆ Activity:

1. Shuffle the cards. Place them face down in neat rows.

2. The game begins when one player turns over a card, looks at it, and then turns over another to see if he can find a match. Everyone should be able to see the pictures on the cards.

3. If a match is made, the player keeps the cards and gets another turn. If no match is made, both cards are replaced face down and the next person takes a turn.

4. The player with the most cards at the end of the game "wins." But don't emphasize the winning part—just have fun!

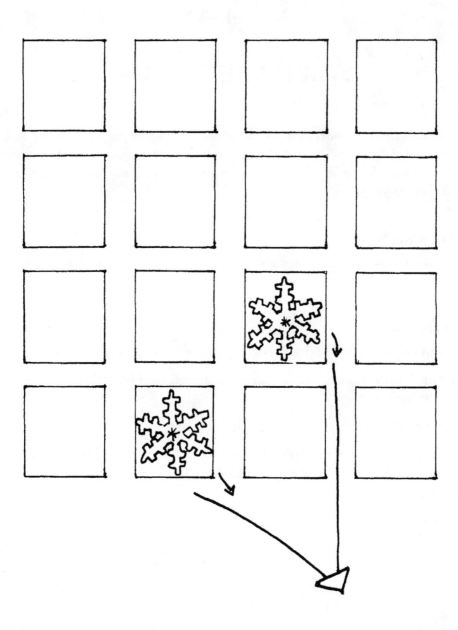

❧ 4 ❧

ALPHABET BOOK

This project—which includes a cheery rhyme and pictures for your child to cut and color—is one of the easiest, most effective ways to teach the sounds and shapes of the letters. Encourage her to "read" the book with you often and soon the letters will become friends that she recognizes.

☞ What You Need:

Alphabet Pictures–large (page 36), cardstock, ruler, colored markers, scissors, glue, hole punch, yarn or rings

✄ To Prepare:

1. Cut twenty-eight 5½- by 8½-inch pages out of cardstock.

2. Punch three holes down the side of each page, then bind them together with yarn or rings.

3. Write My Alphabet Book on the front cover.

4. Write one letter of the alphabet, from *a* to *z*, on each right-hand page. When you open the book you will see a letter on the right and a blank page on the left.

☆ **Activity 1:**

1. Invite your child to color, cut out, and glue the apple Alphabet Picture on the inside front cover opposite the letter *a*. When the book is finished, letters will appear on the right, pictures on the left.

   Note: For a very young child, prepare the book yourself and introduce it completed.

2. Say the letter's sound (page 51) and refer to it throughout the day. Encourage your child to point out things that begin with that letter.

3. Take your time. Do one or more pages daily until the project is done.

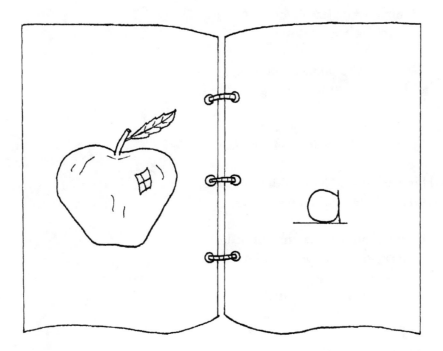

☆ **Activity 2:**

1. Read the book with your child. Point to the letter, say its sound, then point to the corresponding picture and say the rhyme (page 50). Emphasize the first *sound* of the word that represents the letter. Say, "*a, a* is for *apple* so juicy and sweet."

2. Encourage her to "read" the book with you and by herself, often.

Alphabet Rhyme

a is for apple so juicy and sweet,
b is for boots you put on your feet.

c is for cap that keeps off the sun,
d is for dogs that bark, jump, and run.

e is for elephant with a long nose and short tail,
f is for feathers you find on a quail.

g is for games that you like to play,
h is for hands that you wash everyday.

i is for infant who's learning to talk,
j is for jewel—a bright, shiny rock.

k is for kitten who pounces on string,
l is for lips that help you to sing.

m is for melon—a sweet, juicy treat,
n is for napkin that helps you stay neat.

o is for octagon—a shape with eight sides,
p is for pony that takes you on rides.

q is for quilt mother lays on your bed,
r is for roses in yellow, pink, and red.

s is for stars that twinkle at night,
t is for truck so shiny and bright.

u is for umbrella. It keeps you dry in the rain,
v is for violets that grow in the lane.

w is for wind that blows off your hat,
x is for Feli<u>x</u>—the name of my cat.

y is for yarn in a sweater for you, and
z is for zebra you see in a zoo.

A Word About Letter Sounds

Each letter has a *name* <u>and</u> one or more *sounds.* The letter *b,* for example, has the name *bee,* but its *sound* is short and explosive, without any following vowel tone. (Hear the letter sounds: www.paolinimethod.com/downloads) Teach your child the names of the letters, *Aee, Bee, Cee,* etc., but emphasize the phonetic *sounds* of the letters and he will soon be able to decipher words.

Each vowel *(a, e, i, o, u)* represents two or more sounds. Notice the *a* in *c<u>a</u>t, c<u>a</u>ke,* and *f<u>a</u>ther.* To simplify, teach your child the *short* sound of each vowel as demonstrated by these words: *c<u>a</u>t, h<u>e</u>n, p<u>i</u>n, d<u>o</u>g, n<u>u</u>t.* This will give him the tools to begin reading simple words and sentences.

When you say the consonants (all the letters that are not the vowels—*a, e, i, o, u*), try to say just the *sound* of the letter. In our *b* example, say the word *bat.* Now say the *b* sound without the *at* that follows. The letters *b, c, d, g, j, k, p,* and *t* have short, explosive sounds. Try isolating their sounds in the words *<u>b</u>at, <u>c</u>at, <u>d</u>ig, <u>g</u>un, <u>j</u>am, <u>k</u>itten, <u>p</u>in,* and *<u>t</u>op.* The sound for letter *h* is also short, but it is quietly exhaled, as in *<u>h</u>at.* Another short sound is *y.* Say it as in *<u>y</u>arn.*

The sounds for *f, l, m, n, r, s, v, w,* and *z* are held longer. Say them as the first sound in these words: *<u>f</u>ox, <u>l</u>amp, <u>m</u>op, <u>n</u>ut, <u>r</u>un, <u>s</u>it, <u>v</u>ase, <u>w</u>indow, <u>z</u>ebra.* The letter *q* is always followed by *u* and is said *kw* as in *<u>qu</u>iet.* The letter *x* combines two sounds and is said *ks* as in *fo<u>x</u>.*

Note: Letters such as *c* that have more than one sound, as in *<u>c</u>ap* and *<u>c</u>ent;* consonant pairs, such as *<u>sh</u>ip, <u>ch</u>ess, <u>th</u>e, <u>th</u>ink,* and *<u>wh</u>en;* and long vowel sounds in words such as *c<u>a</u>k<u>e</u>, r<u>ai</u>n, f<u>ee</u>d, s<u>ea</u>l, t<u>i</u>m<u>e</u>, h<u>igh</u>, fl<u>y</u>, h<u>o</u>m<u>e</u>, b<u>oa</u>t, sn<u>ow</u>,* and *m<u>u</u>l<u>e</u>* are presented in later chapters.

❧ 5 ❧

ONE-WORD PICTURE BOOKS

Make these simple books with a theme—such as sea shells, hats, flowers, carpentry tools, vehicles, farm animals, insects, cats, or musical instruments—to help your child associate words with things and expand his vocabulary. Invite him to construct the booklets with you or build them yourself to offer as a surprise!

☞ **What You Need:**

Paper or cardstock, pictures, scissors, glue, colored markers, hole punch, yarn

✄ **To Prepare:**

1. Cut paper or cardstock into rectangular pages, ten is a good number. To keep interest high, vary page size and color in different books. Punch holes down the side.

2. Glue pictures or draw simple illustrations onto one side of every page except one, which will make the back cover.

3. Arrange the pages as they will be in the finished book. Write the name of the each item on the page opposite the picture. Use colored markers to add interest.

4. Bind the pages with yarn tied through the holes.

Examples:

When our first child, Christopher, was two, I made him a set of seven little books decorated with pictures cut from clothing catalogs. They were titled "red clothes," "yellow clothes," "blue clothes," etc. Each book was written with matching colored marker and tied with matching embroidery thread. Formed with quarter sheets of white paper, they had pictures on the left pages and the words *red dress, red shoes, red pants,* etc. on the right pages.

I read these simple books with Christopher repeatedly, then reused them with our daughter, Angela.

☆ **Activity:**

Read the books with your child. Be attentive as he "reads" them to you.

❧ 6 ❧

ALPHABET TRAIN

Youngsters love this stylized bulletin board project. Make one or more cars daily—letting your child's level of interest guide your pace—to help her memorize the letters' shapes and sounds.

☞ **What You Need:**

Construction paper, glue, scissors, colored markers or crayons, pictures for each letter of the alphabet or Alphabet Pictures–small (page 36)

✂ **To Prepare:**

1. Decide on the size of your Alphabet Train. Use whole, half, or quarter pieces of construction paper to make the cars.

2. Begin by building the engine. Simply add a smoke stack, window, headlight, and cattle guard at the front of a regular car, as shown.

3. Tape the engine on an open stretch of wall. Make sure you have enough room to complete all twenty-six cars of the Alphabet Train.

☆ **Activity 1:**

1. With your child, decorate the first train car with markers and construction paper in contrasting colors. Decorate only the borders. Leave the center open.

2. Use a bright marker to write the alphabet letter *a* on a piece of construction paper. Tape it to the top center of the car.

3. Say the sound of the letter and encourage her to say it several times. "This is *a*. Can you say *a*? *a* lives in this car. Now let's put the wheels on the *a* car."

4. Show her how to glue two circles for wheels at the bottom. Then tape the *a* car behind the engine, linking it with a thin strip of construction paper.

5. Work through the alphabet in order—one letter per car—until all the cars are built. Stop each session while her interest is still high, so she will be eager to return to the project another day.

☆ **Activity 2:**

1. With your child, draw or cut out pictures of things that begin with the letter in the Alphabet Train car you are making.

   Note: Make sure to choose pictures that sound like the first letter. A pheasant would go under *f* not *p*. Better yet, don't use it at all.

2. Invite her to tape the pictures onto the car.

3. Point to the letter and say its sound. Point to a picture and say its name, *"a, apple."* Ask her to do the same. Repeat for all the items in the car.

☆ **Activity 3:**

Another day, when several of the Alphabet Train cars are completed, play this little game to reinforce the letters' sounds.

1. Ask your child to find one of the Alphabet Train cars, for example, "Can you find the *d* car?"

2. With her, point to each of the pictures and say, "*d* duck, *d* dog, *d* desk, *d* dove."

3. Repeat with other letters.

Examples:

Here are some picture ideas:

a: apple, ant, aster, alligator, ax, anchor, antler, ankle, amethyst, alpaca, anteater, antelope, abacus, Africa, address, albatross, amber, anaconda, animals, astronaut

b: butterfly, basket, banana, bear, bed, bat, bunny, bee, bird, baby, ball, ballerina, banjo, barn, bell, bench, boot, bottle, box, bracelet, bread, broom, button, bubbles, brush

c: cow, car, corn, cat, camera, crayon, candle, candy, coin, camel, crown, cabin, cactus, cake, can, cane, canoe, carrot, carpet, cave, coat, cocoon, coin, compass, cone, crow, cup, cupcake, cube

d: dime, deer, duck, dog, dragon, door, doll, dandelion, dove, dinosaur, dad, daisy, daffodil, desert, desk, dessert, dice, diamond, dish, diver, dollar, dolphin, donkey, dominoes, dove, drum, drill

e: egg, elephant, engine, elk, envelope, eggplant, emerald, elbow, elevator, eleven, elm, elf

f: flag, flower, fish, fern, fork, fire, fairy, fan, fence, fawn, finger, face, falcon, farm, father, feather, feet, fence, ferret, five, flamingo, four, frog, fruit, funnel, fur

g: goat, glass, golf ball, grapes, grasshopper, guitar, gift, gold, goose, game, garden, gate, geyser, gill, globe, glove, glue, gorilla, gown, grandmother, grapefruit, green h: horse, hoe, helicopter, hand, hammer, hat, hen, heart, hummingbird, hair, hamster, harp, head, hedgehog, heel, hexagon, hive, hip, honey, hoof, horn, hose, house, hyena, hut

i: insect, ink, iguana, Indian, igloo, Indiana, India, indigo, impala, inch, infant, Italy

j: jet, jacket, jam, jellybeans, jade, jail, jug, jeep, jaguar, jump rope, Japan, jar, January, jay, jeans, jester, juggle, juice, Jupiter

k: key, kangaroo, ketchup, kite, kitten, Kentucky, kettle, king, kayak, kelp, kidney, kimono, kitchen, kiwi, koala, koi

l: lettuce, lizard, lion, lemon, leaf, ladybug, lamp, lamb, locket, licorice, lace, ladder, ladle, lake, lantern, lava, lawn, leaf, leg, leopard, library, light bulb, lighthouse, lime, lips, llama, lobster, log, lunch, lollipop

m: money, map, monkey, mushroom, mustard, mirror, marble, mop, macaroni, magnet, man, manatee, Mars, March, mask, mat, maze, meat, melon, Mercury, microscope, milk, mitten, mom, moon, moose, moth, motorcycle, mouse, muffin, mouth

n: nut, newspaper, needle, nickel, nest, necklace, nurse, net, neck, nail, napkin, nutmeg, nectarine, Neptune, newt, nightgown, nine, noodle, nose, notebook, November, nutria

o: octopus, octagon, olive, otter, ostrich, ox, ocelot

p: popcorn, plate, pillow, plane, pen, pig, peach, pineapple, pine cone, paddle, pail, paintbrush, pajamas, palace, palm, pan, pants, panda, paper, parrot, pasta, peach, peacock, peanut, pear, peas, pelican, pencil, penguin, penny, pentagon, pepper, pie, pin, pink, pizza, pocket, plate, poodle, poppy, popsicle, porcupine, potato, pretzel, pumpkin, pyramid, puzzle, purse, puppy

q: quilt, queen, quartz, quail, question mark, quarter, quiet, quiver, quart

r: rock, rug, river, red, ring, rabbit, radish, ribbon, roadrunner, raccoon, racket, radio, rain, raisin, rake, raspberry, rat, rattlesnake, recipe, rectangle, refrigerator, reindeer, rhinoceros, rice, road, robin, robot, rocket, roll, roof, rooster, roots, rope, rose s: snake, snow, sunflower, sun, skirt, slug, snowman, sand, soap, seal, spoon, sail, salad, salt, sandwich, saw, scarf, scissors, screw, seaweed, seeds, September, seven, silk, silver, sisters, skeleton, skunk, sky slipper, smile, snail, sock, sofa, soup, spider, spatula, sponge, squash, stamp, starfish, stars, stick, strawberry, stump, submarine, suitcase, sunflower, swan, sword, swimsuit

t: table, tub, top, tiger, teaspoon, telephone, toast, tree, toad, tent, tail, tadpole, tambourine, tape, target, tea, taxi, teacher, tears, television, ten, tie, tire, toaster, toe, tomato, tongue, tooth, towel, toys, train, truck, tuba, turkey, tutu, twenty, twins, two

u: umbrella, underwear, up, under, uncle, undershirt

v: velvet, Venus, volcano, violin, vanilla, vacuum, violet, vest, vegetable, Valentine, valley, van, vase, vine, vinegar, vulture

w: walnut, walrus, watermelon, wing, worm, windmill, wagon, wolf, waist, wallet, wand, washer, wasp, wastebasket, watch, water, waterfall, wave, weasel, web, wig, window, witch, wolf, wolverine, woman, wood, woodpecker

x: ax, wax, ox, box, fox

y: yarn, yellow, yam, yeast, yawn, yak, yacht, yard, yell, yogurt, yolk, yo-yo, yucca, yes

z: zebra, zero, zoo, zipper, zinnia, zigzag, zither, zucchini

LETTER TREE

Make this project for more fun letter practice. Build it with construction paper on a bulletin board or wall or, as described in the variation, on a real tree branch. Either way, it gives your child something special to look forward to each day—adding a new leaf to the tree. If he is very familiar with the letters, he may prefer to do the project all at once. For young children, it's nice to focus on one letter at a time.

☞ **What You Need:**

Construction paper, plain paper, scissors, tape, basket or box, envelope, colored marker

✄ **To Prepare:**

1. Cut brown construction paper to make a tree with branches. Tape it on a bulletin board or wall.

2. Cut large yellow, orange, brown, red, and green leaf shapes. Place the paper leaves into a basket or box.

3. Write the letters of the alphabet on small slips of paper and place them in an envelope or small box.

☆ **Activity:**

1. Invite your child to choose a leaf.

2. Ask him to close his eyes and choose a letter from the envelope or small box. Have him open his eyes and say the letter's sound. Say it with him if he needs help.

3. With a colored marker, write the letter on the leaf. Encourage him to say its sound again.

4. Invite him to tape the Letter Leaf on the Letter Tree.

5. Together, point to and say the sounds of all the Letter Leaves on the tree.

Variation:

Make the Letter Tree using a real tree branch instead of paper. You will need a branch, thread, a hole punch, and something to keep the branch upright, such as a chunk of clay or a container full of pebbles. Secure the branch in the clay or pebbles, then proceed with the Activity directions, with this change: punch a hole in the top of each paper leaf and tie it to the branch with thread.

✌ 8 ✌

LETTER CARDS

Letter Cards are traceable alphabet letters made by gluing cornmeal or sand onto card-stock. Alternately, you can make these using cardboard or felt letters. Build the Letter Cards all at once or include your child in the project by making one or more each day.

Once you have a full set of Letter Cards, do Activities 1, 2, and 3 to help her learn the letter sounds and how to trace their shapes. Save the Letter Cards in a basket for future lessons.

☞ **What You Need:**

Red and blue construction paper or cardstock, pencil, scissors, glue, cornmeal or sand, basket

✂ **To Prepare: Letter Cards**

1. Cut twenty-one cards out of red construction paper or cardstock. Cut five cards out of blue construction paper or cardstock. Larger cards work best for younger children, smaller cards for older students.

2. Use a pencil to mark a baseline one-third up from the bottom of each card. Write the alphabet letters on the lines, one per card. Write the vowels *(a, e, i, o, u)* on the blue cards. Write all the other letters (the consonants) on the red cards.

3. Trace a thick band of glue over the letters and sprinkle with cornmeal or sand. Let dry completely.

4. Shake off the excess grit. These are your Letter Cards. Keep them in a special basket that becomes their "home."

☆ **Activity 1: Letter Sounds**

1. Set out a Letter Card. Trace the shape of the letter with your fingers and say its sound (A Word About Letter Sounds, page 51). Make sure to trace the letter as you would write it. Do this twice, then invite your child to repeat your actions. Set the card aside.

2. Choose another Letter Card and repeat.

3. Do this activity with one or more Letter Cards each day until your child can trace the letters and say their sounds by herself.

☆ **Activity 2: Can You Find *a*?**

1. Set out three or more Letter Cards. Say the sound of one letter and ask your child to point to it.

2. Mix the Letter Cards and ask for a different letter.

3. Repeat the activity using different sets of Letter Cards. Do this over days or weeks until she can identify the letters by sound.

☆ Activity 3: What Is This?

1. Set out three or more Letter Cards. This time, instead of you saying the sound of a letter, point to the cards one by one and ask her to tell you their sounds.

2. Repeat the activity in short sessions using different sets of Letter Cards until she can say each letter's sound with confidence.

Note: If she has difficulty with this, calmly put the lesson away and present Activities 1 and 2 at another time. Be patient and don't worry. She just needs more practice.

ᴀ 9 ᴀ

LETTER CARDS GAMES

This collection of pre-reading activities works with the preceding lesson, reinforcing the letters' sounds, which are the building blocks of our language. Playing these games in short daily sessions helps your child to think of the letters as friends. Learning their sounds prepares him to read. Tracing them prepares him to write.

☞ **What You Need:**

Letter Cards (page 62) in their "home" basket, another basket

Note: If you don't have Letter Cards, write the letters (consonants red, vowels blue) on 3-inch by 5-inch index cards and substitute.

☆ **Activity 1: Hello *a!***

Saying hello to the Letter Cards one at a time, tracing them, and then saying goodbye to each while putting it away delights young children. Invite your child to sit with you on the floor and bring out a few letters at a time. Let his interest guide how long you do the activity. This little game can be played over and over for weeks or months until he can easily say the letter *sounds* (page 51) and trace them.

1. Set out the *a* Letter Card. Say, "Hello *a!*" (Make sure you use the letter's *sound.*) Set out the *b, c, d,* and *e* Letter Cards in a row. Say hello to each one: "Hello *b,* Hello *c,*" etc.

2. Once all five Letter Cards are placed, ask your child to trace one of the letters, "Can you trace the *d?*" Have him trace the letter with his fingers and say its sound, *d.* Repeat with the other letters.

3. After all the letters have been traced, either add another row of letters under the first and repeat the naming and tracing actions of Step 2, or conclude the activity this way: Say, "It's time for our letter friends to go home. Goodbye *a.*" Pick up the a Letter Card. Wave goodbye to it and put it in its home basket. Repeat for each of the remaining Letter Cards.

4. Repeat with different letters on other days. Be attuned to your child's level of attention. Conclude the lessons before he loses interest.

☆ **Activity 2: Bring Me *a!***

Do this activity once your child is proficient with Activity 1. It reinforces his knowledge, checks his proficiency, and adds another level of difficulty, because he must identify the letters by sound. His desire to move is engaged by having him trot back and forth between you and the Letter Cards, and he will feel a sense of accomplishment as he brings each one.

1. Set a few, half, or all of the Letter Cards out in rows on the floor. Sit across the room with the Letter Card basket.

2. Say, "Phillip, can you bring me *f*?" Make sure you use the letter's *sound*. When he brings the *f* Letter Card, thank him and place it in its basket.

3. Continue asking for letters until all the Letter Cards have been brought. Keep the activity fun. If he makes a mistake, note that he needs more practice and review the letter another time.

☆ **Activity 3: Letters on Vacation**

This game has two purposes. Hidden behind the fun of returning the Letter Cards home from "vacation" is a test of your child's ability to correctly identify and say each Letter Card's sound. Be sure to keep the game upbeat. If he gives the incorrect sound for a Letter Card or has trouble remembering it, note the letter and review it another time.

1. Place the Letter Cards into a bag or upside down in a basket or box different from their "home." Place the empty Letter Card basket across the room or in a different room.

2. Sit with your child and the Letter Cards. Explain that the cards are taking a vacation, but now it's time for them to go home. Take them out one at a time and say, "What is this?" He answers, "This is *r*." You say, "Can you please take *r* home?" He carries the Letter Card to its home basket. Repeat with the other letters.

3. Celebrate when all the letters have returned home.

Examples:

Invite your child to find a spot on a map where the Letter Cards are vacationing. Choose a state, such as Arizona, Hawaii, or Maine; or choose a country, such as France, Canada, or Japan. Discuss a little about the place the Letter Cards are visiting, then have him bring them home one by one.

❧ 10 ❧

TRACE⸗A⸗SHAPE

This activity encourages your child to use a pencil, become familiar with simple shapes, experiment with color, and express her creativity. Most importantly, it strengthens the muscles of her hand and fingers, thereby improving her fine motor control in preparation for writing. Once she has made ten pages, cut a construction paper cover and staple the sheets together at the side. Then invite her to decorate the cover of her booklet.

I recommend you purchase a set of soft-lead art pencils for this activity because they lay down a lovely thick line of color with little pressure.

☞ **What You Need:**

Cardboard, box cutter, ruler, white and colored paper, soft-lead colored pencils (page 35), tray

✂ **To Prepare:**

1. Use the box cutter to cut three 5½-inch squares out of cardboard.

2. Draw, then cut out a square, circle, and triangle from the centers of the cardboard pieces. Cut cleanly, so the edges are smooth. You'll be using the frames for the first activities. Reserve the cutout inner shapes for use in Variation 3.

3. Cut a stack of 5½- by 5½-inch white and colored paper. This is Trace-a-Shape paper.

4. Arrange the cardboard stencils, paper, and colored pencils on a tray.

How to Hold a Pencil

Pinch the pencil with the thumb and first finger just above the line where the paint meets the sharpened wood tip. Let the pencil rest on the first joint of the middle finger, as shown below. This is called the three-fingered grip. Left-handers use a similar position but should grip the pencil a bit higher so they can see over and around their hand.

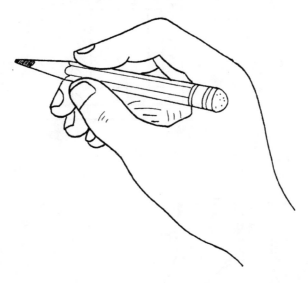

☆ **Activity:**

Demonstrate, then invite your child to follow these steps:

1. Place a piece of Trace-a-Shape paper on a table. Lay one of the cardboard stencils over the paper. Press down on the stencil with the left hand (reverse, if your child is left-handed) and hold a colored pencil in the right hand, showing her how to use the three-fingered grip, as described above. Trace around the inside of the shape with the pencil. Do this slowly so she can see how to press against the edge of the stencil to create the shape.

   Note: Draw the *circle* starting at the top and going around in a counter-clockwise direction, as if you were writing an *a* or an *o*. Draw the *square* beginning in the top left corner and going right.

2. Remove the stencil. Admire the shape and say its name. Place the paper aside and invite your child to try one with a different colored pencil.

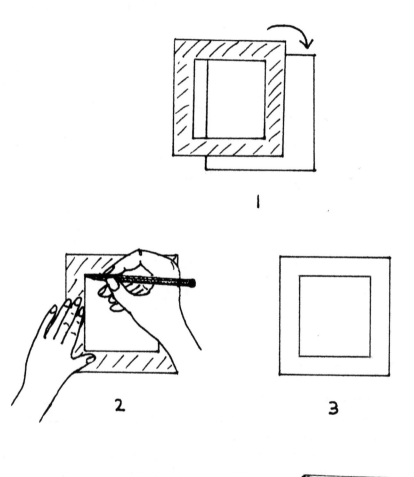

1

2   3

3. Once ten pages are finished, cut a colorful construction paper cover and staple down the side to make a book. Write "trace a shape" on the cover and invite your child to decorate it. Be attentive and admire her work as she shows it to you.

Variation 1:

Trace inside the stencil. Fill in the center of the shape using a pencil of contrasting color. Demonstrate how to make light, down strokes that move from left to right in several rows across the shape. Practicing this pattern prepares your child to make the lines that form letters and familiarizes her with the left-to-right pattern of writing. Invite her to make lots of these pretty designs.

Variation 2:

Trace inside the stencil. Remove the cardboard and put a different shape on the paper. Trace the second shape over the first. Fill in the spaces using different colors. Invite your child to experiment with this on her own.

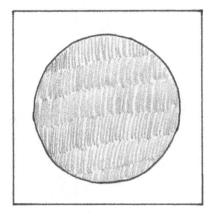

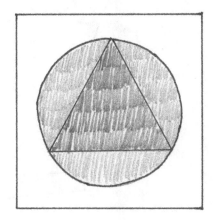

Variation 1   Variation 2

Variation 3:

Bring out the reserved shapes that you cut from cardboard in the To Prepare section on page 68. Demonstrate how to trace around the cutout shapes. Use the non-writing hand to hold a shape firmly in place. Cross the pencil over the holding hand and begin to draw. Draw around as far as you can—until blocked by the holding hand—then lift the pencil and reach it under the holding hand and complete the shape. Let your child experiment with this new way of making shapes.

Variation 4:

Prepare and introduce other shapes, such as oval, rectangle, right triangle, and pentagon.

Variation 4

❧ 11 ❧

MAGIC RUBBINGS

*Set some thin items under a piece of paper. Color with crayon or pencil and . . . voila!
The shapes magically appear. Not only is this activity fun, it's another way for your child
to strengthen his fingers and gain motor control in preparation for writing.*

☞ **What You Need:**

Paper, crayons or colored pencils, thin items such as snippets of construction
paper, string, lace, or leaves

☆ **Activity:**

1. Have your child choose one or more items for his rubbing.

2. Work on a hard surface such as a table. Arrange the objects on a piece of
   paper. Lay a second piece of paper on top.

3. Demonstrate how to secure the paper with the non-writing hand and how
   to hold the pencil or crayon using the three-fingered grip (page 69). Use
   downward shading strokes that move from left to right in several rows
   across the shape, mimicking the pattern that is used in writing. Invite him
   to make a rubbing of his own.

✣ 12 ✣

LINES OF WRITING

Letters are written with vertical, horizontal, and slanted lines, along with curves and circles. This activity prepares your child to write by introducing these shapes individually. It also gives her practice holding a pencil with the three-fingered grip (page 69).

Introduce different Lines of Writing over days or weeks. Give your child ample opportunity to practice each before introducing a new line. Activities 1 through 4 prepare her for the last activity, Lines of Writing Booklet, which is the final step before she writes the letters of the alphabet.

☞ **What You Need:**
   Plain paper, large writing paper (page 36), soft-lead colored pencils (page 35)

☆ **Activity 1: Lines**
   1. Before you begin writing, have your child experience the direction of a vertical line with her whole body. Together, raise your arms overhead and bring them straight down in front of you. Do this several times, saying *down* each time you lower your arms.

   2. Invite her to choose a colored pencil and show her how to hold it using the three-fingered grip (page 69).

   3. Take a piece of plain paper and show her how to draw *down* lines with large strokes. Raise the pencil at the end of each stroke, go back to the top of the paper, and go down again. Say *down* each time.

   4. On other days, do steps 1 and 3 for lines that go *across* (horizontal) and *slant* (diagonal).

Variation:

Two other fun ways to learn the lines of direction is to trace them in finger paint or draw them on a big sheet of paper with a large paintbrush.

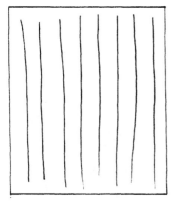
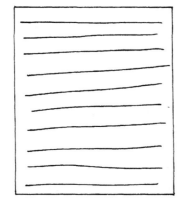
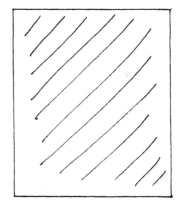

☆ **Activity 2: Curved Lines**

1. To help your child experience the feeling of a curved line, have her curl up on the floor in a *C* shape. Then have her stand up and draw the shapes in the air with large sweeping motions of her arms. Make curves that go to the right and to the left. Say *curve* with each movement.

2. Take a piece of plain paper and demonstrate how to draw large *curve* lines with a pencil. Show her how to make curves that face both directions, saying *curve* each time. Try making big curvy snakes.

☆ Activity 3: Circles

1. Have a circle day! Try some of these activities to highlight the concept of circles.

   Examples:

   - Together, make big circles with your arms.

   - Hold hands and dance in a circle.

   - Hunt to find things that have circle shapes.

   - Suggest she draw a sun, an orange, or a plate filled with round cookies.

   - Have her trace around the bottom of a can, glass, or cup.

   - Invite her to cut circles out of playdough with a biscuit cutter, upside-down glass, or empty can.

   - Demonstrate, then have her make circle prints by dipping the end of a cardboard toilet roll in paint and pressing it on paper.

   - Cut a potato and carrot in half and show her how to make paint-print flowers by printing a large potato circle in the middle and surrounding it with small carrot circles for petals.

2. Show her how to draw *circle* shapes—both clockwise and counterclockwise—with a pencil on a plain sheet of paper. Encourage her to make large and small ones, and remember to have her say *circle*.

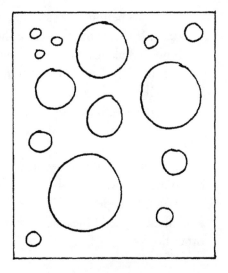

☆ **Activity 4: Mix It Up!**

Now mix it up! After your child has had lots of practice on her own, try these activities:

- Ask her to draw different Lines of Writing: circle, down, slant, curve, . . . etc. Remember, whatever she draws is OK. If you see more instruction is needed, save it for another day. Just watch to see what she understands and how her pencil control is progressing. Keep it fun!

- Trade places. You take the paper and pencil, then have her tell you what to draw.

- Draw a Line of Writing and ask her to name it. When she can both correctly make and name the lines, you know she has mastered this activity.

☆ **Activity 5: Lines of Writing Booklet**

Once your child is familiar with the Lines of Writing, give her a sheet of large writing paper (page 36) cut so that five lines are showing. Have her fill at least one sheet for each of the Lines of Writing: down, across, slant, curves, and circles. If she wants to do more, that's great. If she is not inter-ested, just put the paper away and return to the activity another day.

Note: To help her get started, draw a row of dashed lines for her to trace. If this is the first time she has written on lined paper, show her how to make each "down" line fit between the guide lines and "sit on the line." To keep interest high, suggest she use a different colored pencil on each row. Encourage her to use the three-fingered grip on her pencil and say "down" each time she writes a line. Follow this pattern for the other shapes.

Come back to this activity on subsequent days and save the pages as she completes them. Once she has a set of five to ten pages, cut a piece of construction paper for the cover and staple the pages together to make a booklet. Write "Lines of Writing" on the cover and place it with her other books.

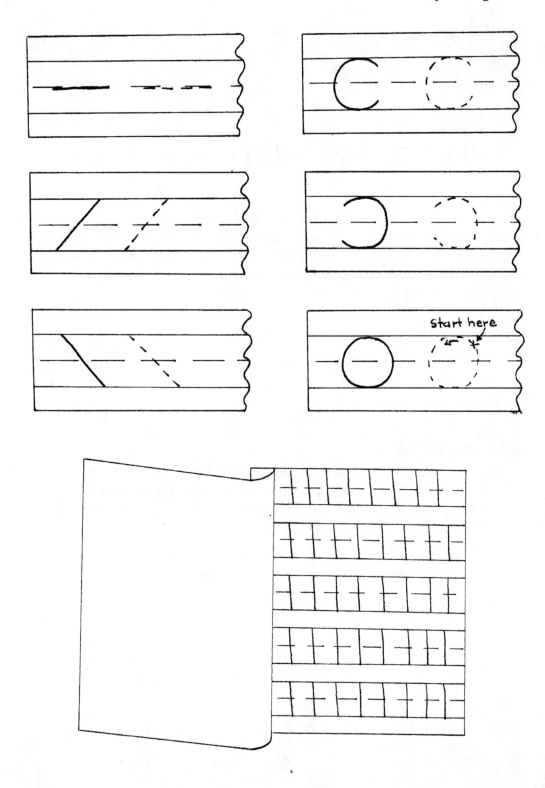

৵ 13 ৵

TRACE AND WRITE: LETTERS

This great project teaches your child how to write the letters. Keep the activity fun by having him trace and write one or more letters each day in short sessions; let his interest guide the speed at which you progress. Some children will do many pages in a day, others will do one or two. Either way, a little daily effort is all it takes for him to progress, so encourage him to practice and watch his writing improve.

☞ What You Need:

Letter Cards (page 62), large writing paper (page 36), Alphabet Pictures–small (page 36), construction paper, glue, ruler, scissors, soft-lead red and blue pencils, two baskets

✄ To Prepare:

1. Cut six sheets of multi-colored construction paper into twenty-six 2⅜- by 9-inch strips. Place the strips into a basket. These will be the colored backing that pictures and writing strips will be glued on and will eventually form the pages of a booklet.

2. Cut twenty-six 6-inch strips of large writing paper. Cut the width to include the upper and lower guide lines, as illustrated.

3. Print out the twenty-six Small Alphabet Pictures. Cut the pictures apart and place them in a basket.

☆ **Activity:**

Demonstrate the following steps as needed until your child can trace and write the letters by himself. Write the consonants in red and the vowels in blue.

1. Invite your child to choose a picture from the basket. Have him say its name and find the matching Letter Card. Trace over the Letter Card with your fingers in the same pattern you write it. Say the Verbal Cues for Letter Writing (page 83) as you trace the letter, then say its sound, for example, "Up and around; up, down; *a.*" Trace it and say its sound a second time. Invite him to trace the letter and say its sound two times himself.

2. Write the letter once on the left side of the lined paper. Make sure he sees where the letter starts and how you form it. Write slowly and say the verbal cues to help him understand how the letter is formed.

3. At this point, you may wish to make a few dashed-line letters for him to trace. Do this with lead pencil. Invite him to continue writing the letter until the strip is full.

4. Demonstrate how to place a thin line of glue around the edge of the lined paper strip and press it onto one of the construction paper strips. Align the right edges. Suggest he color the matching picture and glue it onto the left side of the construction paper strip, as shown.

5. Invite him to choose another letter and repeat steps 1–4 to make another Trace and Write Letter strip.

Note: The letter *q* is always followed by the letter *u* in English. Explain this to your child and have him write *qu* when he chooses the *q* picture.

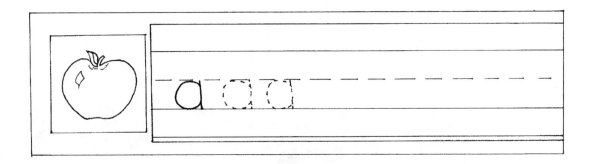

Don't be discouraged if your child's first attempts are clumsy. He will improve with practice. Congratulate him on his efforts and save the strips in a folder or envelope until he has completed one strip for each letter of the alphabet. This may take days or weeks. That's fine. Be patient and encourage him to do a strip or two each day. Help him arrange the strips in alphabetical order and form them into one or two books by punching two holes at the side and binding with yarn. Title the book "Trace and Write Letters."

a b c d e f g h i j k l m n

o p q r s t u v w x y z

Verbal Cues for Writing the Letters:

Take special note of the handwritten *a* and *g,* which differ noticeably from the font used below:

a—up and around, up, down
b—down, up and around
c—up and around
d—up and around, up, down
e—across, up and around
f—curve, straight down, across
g—up and around, up, down and curve
h—down, up, over and down
i—down, dot
j—down, curve, dot
k—down, slant, slant
l—down
m—down, up and over, down, up and over, down
n—down, up and over, down
o—up and around
p—down, up and around
q—up and around, up, down
r—down, up and over
s—up and curve and curve again
t—down and across
u—down, curve, up, down
v—slant down, slant up
w—slant down, slant up, slant down, slant up
x—slant, slant
y—slant, big slant
z—across, slant, across

☙ 14 ☙

KENNETH'S SQUISHY LETTERS

This delightfully messy project helps your child understand the letters' shapes. Don't be surprised if she asks to do it again and again!

☞ What You Need:

Plastic table cloth or sheet of plastic (such as an old shower curtain), instant mashed potato flakes, water, salad oil, bowl, food color (optional)

✂ To Prepare:

1. Cover a table with a protective cover or provide a large tray to work on.

2. Make a potato paste by mixing 2 cups potato flakes, 2¼ cups water, and 2 tablespoons salad oil. Add more or less water as needed. The dough should be thick enough to hold its shape but soft enough to mold. Knead in food color (optional).

   Note: You could use homemade or purchased flour, salt, and water modeling dough instead of the potato paste.

☆ Activity:

1. Show your child how to roll the potato paste into "snakes" and form them into letters.

2. Encourage her to make lots of different letters and say their sounds.

3. When all the paste has been formed into letters, invite her to squish it through her fingers and swirl it in patterns. If you didn't add food color before, add a few drops now. It's fun to watch it blend into the white goo.

4. When she is finished with the activity, have her scrape the paste into a bowl and dump it into the trash.

Variation:

1. Spoon the paste into a cake decorator's bag equipped with a large tip or none at all. A small plastic bag with one corner snipped off also works well.

2. Demonstrate how to squeeze the bag to press out a line of paste. Have your child practice making lines (the letter *l*), then suggest she try making other letters. Encourage her to form the letters correctly; for example, *t* is written with a down stroke and then across, not from the bottom up.

3. Encourage her to write lots of letters all over the tablecloth. Give assistance if required. Additionally, let her experiment making lines, squiggles, and circles. Refill the bag when necessary.

✣ 15 ✣

LABEL THE HOUSE

This lesson is a great way to share in your child's learning experience. Play this game once he understands that printed words represent things. As he watches you write the names of household items, he learns that familiar letters form words.

☞ What You Need:

Cardstock or construction paper, scissors, colored markers

✂ To Prepare:

Cut cardstock or construction paper into rectangular cards.

☆ Activity:

1. Sit with your child. Have the cards and the colored markers at hand. Explain that everything in the house has a name that can be written. Ask him to point to an object and say its name. Then have him watch as you write the word on a card.

2. Ask him to take the card and place it next to the item it names.

Repeat this activity for as long as your child shows interest. Keep the cards in place for a few days and refer to them often.

FIVE SPECIAL FRIENDS

This special lesson helps unlock the mystery of reading. Do this project as soon as your child knows the sounds of the letters. Repeat Activity 1 often—over days or weeks—until she is comfortable saying the vowel sounds. When she is ready, introduce Activity 2 and repeat it over many days, until she can blend two-letter sounds easily. Activity 3 blends three-letter sounds. At this point, many children suddenly understand that the blended sounds represent real things, that the letters c-a-t *represent a cat.*

☞ **What You Need:**

Letter Cards (page 62) or slips of paper with letters (blue vowels and red consonants) written on them.

☆ **Activity 1:**

Demonstrate, then invite your child to follow these steps:

1. Set the five blue Letter Cards in a vertical line as shown—*a, e, i, o, u.* These are the Five Special Friends.

2. Point to the letters, one-by-one, starting with *a.* Say their sounds as you point to them (A Word About Letter Sounds, page 51). Repeat this several times.

Another day, challenge your child to say the vowels in order with her eyes closed.

☆ **Activity 2:**

1. Ask your child to set out the vowels in a vertical line.

2. Invite her to get a consonant letter and place it in front of the *a*. Let's say she chose the letter *b*. Blend the *b* and the *a* sounds and say *ba* (as in the word *bat)*. Now move the *b* down to rest in front of the *e*. Say *be* (as in the word *bed)*. Continue moving the *b* down until you reach *u*. You will have said *ba, be, bi, bo, bu*. Invite her to try it herself.

3. Have her put the *b* away. Invite her to choose a new consonant Letter Card and repeat step 2.

Activity 1   **Activity 2**

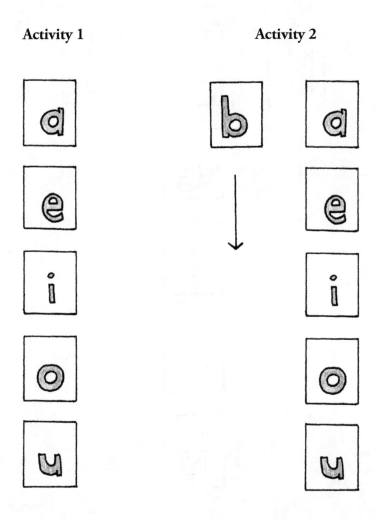

☆ **Activity 3:**

1. Ask your child to set out the vowels in a vertical line.

2. Have her choose one consonant letter, for example *b,* and place it to the left of the vowel, as she did in Activity 2.

3. Introduce a third consonant letter, such as *t.* Place it to the right of the vowel. With your child, move both consonant cards down the vowels and say the blended sounds: *bat, bet, bit, bot, but.* Blend the sounds as if you were reading the words.

4. Invite her to choose other consonant letters and repeat steps 2 and 3.

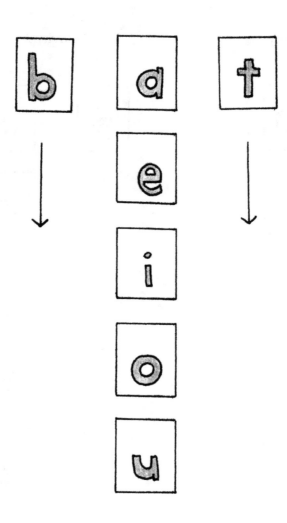

✌ 17 ✌

SHORT VOWEL:

BUILD⹀A⹀WORD

This activity—like the previous lesson, Five Special Friends—is perfect for students on the cusp of reading and may spark that Aha! moment when your child first deciphers words. It then reinforces early reading skills by associating pictures with simple words.

For your convenience, I have included a list of Short Vowel Words in this lesson and a set of Short Vowel Pictures for you to download and print (page 36).

☞ **What You Need:**

Letter Cards (page 62) or slips of paper with letters written on them, Short Vowel Pictures Cards (instructions below), scissors, glue

✂ **To Prepare: Short Vowel Picture Cards**

1. Cut a set of fifty 3½- by 4¼-inch cards from cardstock.

2. Download and print out Short Vowel Pictures–large (page 36). Color, cut, and glue the pictures onto the cards. Make five sets of ten cards each—one set for each vowel. Your child may enjoy helping make these cards.

☆ **Activity:**

1. Bring the basket of Letter Cards to a table or rug.

2. Set out a Short Vowel Picture Card. Say the individual *sounds* (see page 51) of the letters that correspond to the picture, for example, "This is *c-a-t*." Ask your child to find the three Letter Cards—*c, a,* and *t*—and place them next to the picture.

3. Together, point to and say each letter's sound, then say the entire word. "This is *c-a-t, cat.*"

4. Choose a new picture and repeat steps 2 and 3. Build *a* words one day, *e* words another, working your way through the five vowels. If a word requires a double letter, simply write the additional letter on a slip of paper.

Note: For a writing exercise, see Short Vowel: Build-a-Word: Writing (page 105).

 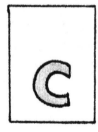 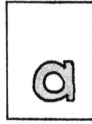 

Short Vowel Words

Refer to this handy list of short vowel words for future projects.

a: Al, ax, add, aft, and, ant, ass, bad, bag, ban, bat, cab, can, cap, cat, dad, dam, Dan, fan, fat, gab, gag, gal, gap, gas, had, hag, Hal, ham, hat, jab, jam, Jan, lad, lag, lap, lax, mad, man, map, mat, Max, nab, nag, Nan, nap, pad, pal, Pam, pan, pat, Pat, rag, ram, ran, rap, rat, sad, sag, Sal, Sam, sap, sat, tab, Tad, tag, tan, tap, Val, van, vat, wag, wax, yak, yam, yap, zap

back, band, bank, bass, blab, black, Brad, brag, bran, brat, camp, can't, cast, clad, clam, clan, clap, crab, crag, cram, damp, dank, drag, drat, fast, flab, flag, flap, flat, flax, Fran, glad, grab, hack, hand, Jack, Kass, lack, lamp, land, last, Mack, mass, mast, pack, pant, pass, past, plan, pram, rack, raft, ramp, Rand, rank, rant, sack, sand, sank, sass, scab, scam, scan, scat, slam, slap, slat, snag, snap, span, spat, stab, stag, Stan, tack, tank, tamp, track, tram, trap, vast

black, bland, blank, brand, Brant, brass, clack, clank, class, crack, craft, cramp, crank, crass, drank, flank, Frank, glass, graft, grand, grant, Grant, grasp, grass, plank, plant, prank, quack, Scamp, scant, scram, scrap, smack, snack, spank, splat, stack, stamp, stand, stank, track, granddad

e: bed, beg, Ben, bet, Bev, Deb, den, Dex, fed, get, hen, Jen, jet, keg, Ken, led, leg, Len, let, Lex, Meg, Mel, men, met, Ned, net, peg, pen, pet, red, Rex, set, Ted, ten, vet, wed, wet, yen, yes, yet, zen, Zed

bell, belt, bend, bent, Bess, best, bled, Bret, deck, deft, dell, dent, desk, fell, fend, fled, Fred, fret, Greg, heck, jell, left, lend, lent, less, melt, mend, mess, neck, Nell, nest, peck, pelt, pest, rend, rent, rest, send, sent, sled, sped, stem, step, tell, tend, tent, test, vend, vent, vest, weft, well, welt, went, west, yell, zest

blend, cleft, crest, dress, press, quest, seven, smell, speck, spell, spend, spent, trend

i: in, bib, bid, big, bin, bit, did, dig, dim, din, dip, fib, fig, fin, fix, gig, gin, him, hip, hit, imp, ink, jig, kid, Kim, kin, kit, lid, Lil, lip, lit, Liv, Liz, nib, nip, pig, pin, Pip, pit, rib, rid, rig, rim, rip, sin, sip, Tim, tin, tip, Viv, wig, win, wit, yip, zip

Bill, blip, brim, Britt, clip, crib, dill, disk, drip, fill, fist, flip, flit, gift, gild, gill, grid, grim, grin, grip, grit, hill, hilt, hint, hiss, Jill, kill, kilt, kink, kiss, Kris, lift, limp, link, lint, list, Mick, milk, mill, mink, mint, miss, mist, mitt, Nick, pick, pill, pink, quip, quit, quiz, Rick, rift, rink, risk, sick, sift, silk, sill, silt, sink, skim, skin, skip, skit, slip, snip, snit, spin, spit, swim, tick, till, tilt, tint, trim, trip, twig, twin, Vick, wick, will, wind, wink

blimp, blink, brick, brink, brisk, click, clink, Clint, crimp, crisp, drift, drill, drink, flick, flint, frill, glint, grill, krill, plink, prick, quick, quill, quilt, script, skill, skimp, spill, splint, split, sprig, sprint, stick, stiff, stilt, stink, stint, tidbit, timid, trick, twill, twist

o: on, ox, Bob, bog, box, cob, cog, con, cop, cot, dog, Don, dot, fog, fox, got, hog, hop, hot, job, jog, Jon, jot, lob, log, lop, lot, mob, mom, mop, nob, nod, odd, off, pod, pop, pot, rob, rod, rot, Roz, sob, sod, sop, Tod, tog, Tom, top, tot

blob, bond, bonk, boss, clod, clog, clop, clot, cock, cost, crop, dock, doll, drop, flog, flop, frog, glob, glop,, honk, lock, loss, lost, moss, plod, plop, plot, pond, prod, rock, Ross, smog, snob, sock, spot, stop, toss, trod, trot

block, clock, clomp, crock, cross, flock, floss, frond, gloss, romp, slot, smock, stock, stomp, pompom

u: up, bud, bug, bum, bun, bus, but, cub, cud, cup, cut, dub, dud, dug, fun, gum, gun, Gus, gut, hug, hum, hut, Jud, jug, jut, lug, mud, mug, mutt, nub, nun, nut, pub, Pug, pun, pup, pus, rub, rug, rum, run, rut, sub, sum, sun, sup, tub, tug, yum buck, buff, bump, bunk, bust, club, cull, drug, drum, duck, dull, dump, dunk, dust, flub, flux, fund, funk, fuss, glum, glut, grub, gull, gulp, gust, huff, hump, hunk, jump, junk, just, luck, lull, lump, muck, muff, mull, must, null, plug, plum, plus, puck, puff, pump, ruff, rump, Russ, rust,

slug, smug, snub, snug, spud, spun, stub, stun, suck, suds, sunk, tuck, yuck, cluck, clump, clunk, crust, drunk, fluff, flunk, gruff, grump, grunt, pluck, plump, plunk, ruckus, scrub, scruff, skunk, slump, snuff, spunk, stuck, stuff, stump, stunk, truck, trunk, trust

Combinations: Alex, apricot, aspen, basket, bitten, blanket, bucket, button, cabinet, cactus, cannon, comic, content, cotton, crumpet, dentist, dragon, droplet, eggplant, elastic, fabric, falcon, fantastic, fragment, gladden, glasses, habit, hidden, jacket, Janet, kitten, lemon, lentil, locket, magnet, mallet, millet, mitten, muffin, mukluk, mullet, napkin, nugget, nutmeg, packet, picnic, planet, plastic, pocket, puffin, pumpkin, puppet, rabbit, racket, ribbon, rocket, rustic, sadden, salad, silken, smitten, socket, sprocket, sudden, tablet, tick-tock, tiptop, trespass, trumpet, visit, windmill, zigzag

BIG BROTHER, LITTLE SISTER

All the projects, so far, have used the small (lower case) letters. This activity introduces the capital letters as big brothers to their little sisters—the small letters.

☞ **What You Need:**

Construction paper, large writing paper (page 36), soft-lead colored pencils, scissors, glue, hole punch, yarn

✂ **To Prepare:**

1. Choose thirteen sheets of brightly-colored construction paper and cut them in half to make twenty-six 6- by 9-inch pages.

2. Cut twenty-six pieces of writing paper to fit on the pages, leaving a space at the top as shown. Glue these onto the construction paper.

3. In the space at the top of the pages, write the capital and small letters as shown. Draw or glue on a small picture of an item that begins with that letter. See Alphabet Picture Ideas (page 56) for help.

☆ **Activity:**

1. Introduce the Big Brother, Little Sister *Aa* page. Explain that the letter *a* (say its short sound—*a* as in *cat*) has a big brother that we call big *A* or capital *A*.

2. Ask your child to write one line of small *a* letters, then let her watch as you write a capital *A* on the second line. Draw a couple of dashed-line capital *A*'s for her to trace. Invite her to fill lines two and three with capital *A*'s.

3. On line four, show her how to write the capital and small letters next to each other. Big brother and little sister now walk together. Ask her to fill lines four and five with *Aa* pairs.

Repeat steps 1–3 for each of the other letters. Keep the activity short and be aware of your child's level of interest. If she is enthusiastic, let her do as many pages as she wants. If she shows moderate engagement, do one page a day. If she is simply not interested at all, put the lesson away and let some days or weeks pass before reintroducing it.

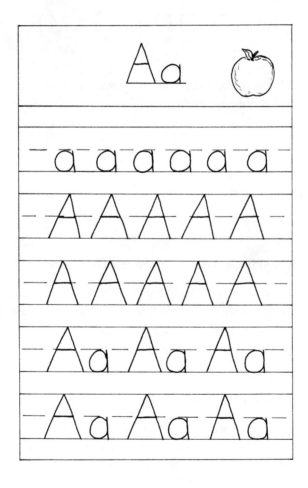

Save the pages as they are completed. After letters *a–m* are finished, cut a construction paper cover, punch three holes down the side, and bind the pages together with yarn. Write *"Aa—Mm"* on the cover. Make a second book when she completes the last half of the alphabet.

✌ 19 ✌

Big A, Little a

Matching Game

Based on a classic children's game, this project reinforces recognition of the letters and their sounds. Your child may enjoy playing it with you, with friends, or as a quiet activity by himself.

☞ What You Need:

Cardstock, ruler, pencil, scissors, red and blue colored markers

✂ To Prepare:

1. Cut cardstock into fifty-two 2½- by 3-inch rectangles.

2. Making the consonants red and the vowels blue, write the capital (big) letters on twenty-six cards, one per card. Next, write the lower case (little) letters on the remaining twenty-six cards.

☆ Activity:

1. Shuffle the cards. Place all the cards face down in neat rows.

2. The game begins when one player turns over a card, looks at it, and says its sound. He then turns over a second card and says its sound to see if he has a match. All players should be able to see the letters on the cards.

3. If a match is made, the player keeps the cards and gets another turn. If no match is made, both cards are replaced face down and the next player takes a turn.

4. Although the player with the most cards at the end "wins," the whole
   point is to practice matching letters and, of course, enjoy the game.

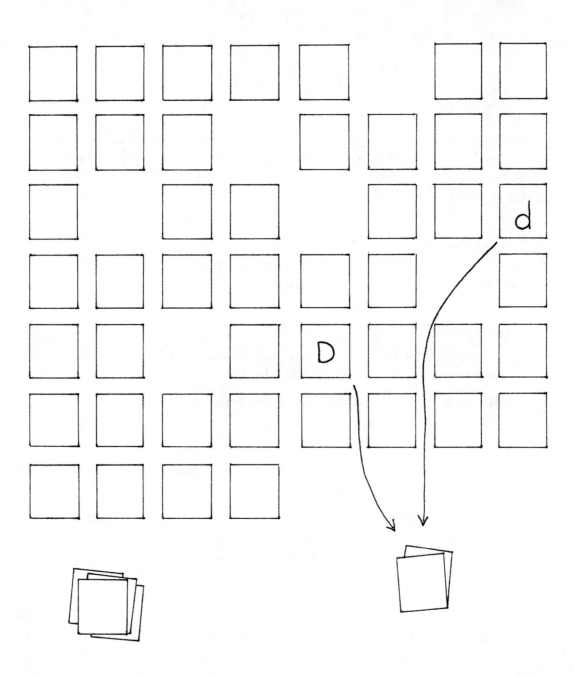

❧ 20 ❧

NAME WRITING

Your child feels a sense of accomplishment and pride when she learns to spell and write her name. Plus, it gives her important writing practice. Encourage her to print her name often on artwork, with a stick in sand, at the bottom of letters to relatives, with finger paint, in mud, or in cake frosting.

☞ **What You Need:**

Letter Cards (page 62) or slips of paper with letters written on them, red and blue soft-lead pencils, large writing paper (page 36)

☆ **Activity 1:**

1. Show your child how to assemble the Letter Cards to make her name. If extra letters are required, simply write them on slips of paper.

2. Mix up the letters and have her try to spell her name by herself.

☆ **Activity 2:**

1. Have your child build her name with the Letter Cards.

2. Demonstrate how to write his name on paper. Use red pencil for the consonants and blue pencil for the vowels *(a, e, i, o, u)*. Say the sound of each letter as you print it. Work slowly, so she can see how the letters are formed. Encourage her to practice writing her name often.

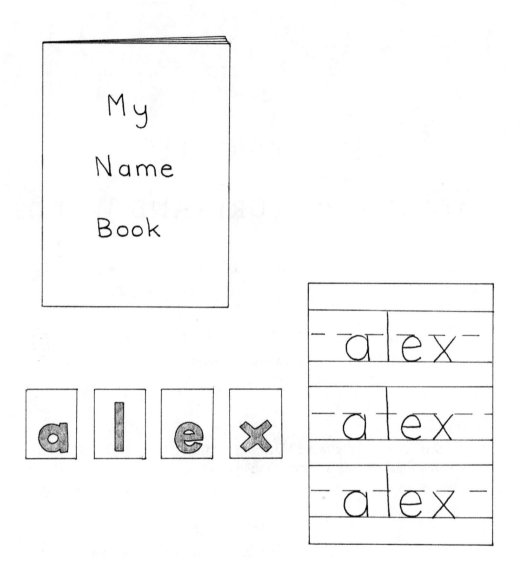

Variation:

Make a Name Book in rainbow colors. Provide seven soft-lead colored pencils to match the rainbow (red, orange, yellow, green, light blue, dark blue (indigo), and purple). Cut writing paper in half or quarters to create seven small pages. Have your child write her name several times per page, using a different colored pencil for each one. When all seven pages are done, arrange them in rainbow order. Cut a construction paper cover, title it "My Name Book," and staple the pages together at the side.

❧ 21 ❧

SHORT VOWEL:

MATCHING PICTURES AND WORDS

Here's a fun project for pre-readers and beginning readers. The first activity requires only that your child be able to differentiate between letters. Activity 2 is for readers.

☞ **What You Need:**

Cardstock, pencil, ruler, scissors, two sets of Short Vowel Pictures–small (page 36), colored pencils or markers, glue

✄ **To Prepare:**

Follow these directions to make Matching Picture and Word Cards (one set with words attached, one without). You may want to make a set for each of the five vowels.

1. Cut twelve 2¼- by 3½-inch rectangles from cardstock.

2. With pencil, draw a thin horizontal line 1 inch above the bottoms of the twelve cards. Set six cards aside, then cut along the lines you drew on the remaining six cards. Save these strips.

3. Color and cut out a matching set of Short Vowel Pictures. Glue one set on the six cards with the bottoms cut off. Glue the second set and on the remaining six cards. Alternately, draw images yourself with colored pencils or markers.

4. On the uncut cards, write the words that match the pictures in the space under the pencil line. Write these words a second time on the loose 1-inch strips.

☆ **Activity 1:**

1. Arrange the uncut set of cards in a vertical line. Set out the cut set of pictures and words at random to the right.

2. Show your child how to pick up a picture and set it next to its twin. Invite him to match all the pictures, then match the words.

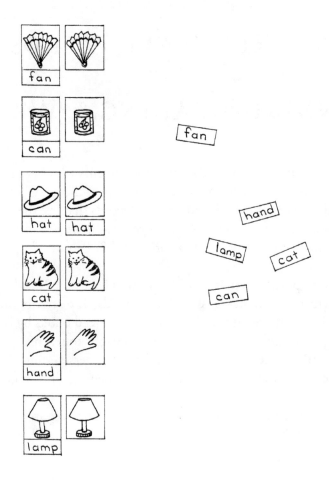

☆ **Activity 2:**

1. Once your child can read, take the divided set of cards and put the pictures in a horizontal line. Place the word strips at random, beneath.

2. Demonstrate how to pick up a word strip, read the word, and then put it under the corresponding picture. Invite him to read and match the remaining word strips.

PART 2

SHORT VOWEL WORDS:

BEGINNING READING & WRITING

The first projects in this section are designed for students who have learned how to decipher a few simple words and can write the letters of the alphabet. The exercises show your child how to make and read books of words that use the "short" sound of each vowel (*a* as in *man, e* as in *hen, i* as in *pig, o* as in *mop,* and *u* as in *nut)* and the common sounds of the consonants as presented in Part 1.

One of the most important activities in this section is Lesson 22, which guides your child through writing five books of short vowel words. The activity provides writing practice, expands her vocabulary, and prepares her to read books by herself. It also builds the habit of working on projects in short sessions to reach a goal. By the time all five booklets are completed, she will have a clear understanding of how simple words are formed and be able to read them easily when she finds them in text.

The rest of the projects in this section expand on the work begun in Lesson 22. Once students reach the end of this unit, they will be comfortable reading short stories and crafting simple sentences.

❧ 22 ❧

SHORT VOWEL:

BUILD-A-WORD: WRITING

This activity is a continuation of Short Vowel: Build-a-Word (page 91). It is an essential exercise that gives your child lots of practice building, writing, and reading short vowel words. Have her do one, two, or three pages a day until she makes a book of ten pages for each of the five vowels.

☞ **What You Need:**
 Letter Cards (page 62), Short Vowel Pictures–Small (page 36), Short Vowel Picture Cards (page 91), large writing paper (page 36), white or colored paper, red and blue soft-lead colored pencils, scissors, glue, stapler

✂ **To Prepare:**
 Your child will make a ten-page book for each vowel. Instructions for making one book are listed below:

1. Cut five sheets of white or colored paper in half to make ten 8½- by 5½-inch rectangles of paper. These will become Build-a-Word Writing Pages.

2. Cut the writing paper into ten 5- by 5½-inch sheets so that four sets of writing lines are available, as shown.

3. Print out a set of Short Vowel Pictures for the vowel you are working with.

☆ **Activity: 1.**

1. Bring the basket of Letter Cards to a table or rug.

2. Set out a Short Vowel Picture Card. Say the individual *sounds* of the word, such as "This is *f-l-a-g*" (A Word About Letter Sounds, page 51). Ask your child to find the four Letter Cards (*f, l, a,* and *g)* and place them next to the picture. If a word requires a duplicate letter, simply write it on a slip of paper.

3. Together, point to and say each letter's sound, then say the entire word. "This is *f-l-a-g, flag.*"

4. With your child watching, write the word on the prepared lined paper, using red pencil for consonants and blue for vowels. Invite her to print the word three times herself.

5. Show her how to place a line of glue around the outer edge of the writing paper and press it onto a 5½- by 8½-inch sheet of plain paper.

6. Ask her to find the matching Short Vowel Picture, cut it out, color it, and then glue it on the top of the Build-a-Word Writing Page. Alternately, suggest she draw her own picture and glue it on. Set the page aside to dry.

7. Invite her to choose another Short Vowel Picture Card and repeat steps 2–6. Write the first word for her each time until her skills improve, so she can see how the letters are formed.

8. When ten pages of *a* words are completed, add a construction paper cover and staple down the sides to form a book. Title the book with your child's name and the vowel: Angela's *a* words, Jason's *e* words, Marvin's *i* words, Abbie's *o* words, or Irene's *u* words. Encourage your child to read the book often.

❧ 23 ❧

SHORT VOWEL:

WORDS I CAN READ

Your child's vocabulary expands as he reads these lists of short vowel words. And he learns that his phonics skills help him decipher new words with confidence.

☞ **What You Need:**

Plain white paper, scissors, ruler, colored paper or cardstock, colored markers, hole punch, string or yarn

✁ **To Prepare:**

1. Measure and cut 2½- by 5½-inch pages from plain paper.

2. Cut a cover from colorful paper or cardstock. Punch two holes in the top of the cover and pages. Loosely bind with string or yarn.

3. Write "Words I Can Read" on the cover with colored marker.

4. At the top of each page, write the title vowel or letter group, as shown in the illustration on page 109 and in the Examples that follow. List the associated words underneath. For variety, use a different colored marker for each page.

☆ **Activity:**

Invite your child to sit and read the booklets to you. Discuss any unfamiliar words and use them in a sentence. Give him a hug and congratulate him for his efforts. Repeat the activity often until he can easily decipher the words.

Variation:

For writing practice, invite your child to copy the word lists onto paper and make his own books.

Examples:

Here are word lists for four separate booklets. Each line of words represents one page.

Book 1

a: jam, nap, bat, flag, gas, camp, cap, fan, hat, wax

e: fed, net, nest, rest, went, well, bed, peg, jet, pet

i: pin, lip, fin, rip, swim, fix, drip, flip, twig, mitten

o: fox, sock, mop, dot, pot, job, lock, box, top, dog

u: mud, dump, nut, button, drum, gum, cut, pup, luck, crust

Book 2

an: and, can, fan, man, pan, ran, tan, van, plan, clan, hand

at: cat, fat, rat, mat, bat, flat, vat, slat, hat, pat, sat

ed: fed, red, bed, wed, led, fled, sled, Ned, Ted

et: get, wet, let, set, bet, met, net, pet, jet, puppet

in: pin, win, tin, fin, bin, twin, grin, kin, spin

op: mop, top, cop, drop, stop, pop, glop, hop, flop, slop

ug: bug, dug, hug, jug, lug, mug, rug, tug, plug, slug

Book 3

ack: sack, lack, track, back, Mack, hack, pack, quack, rack, tack

ast: cast, fast, last, mast, past, vast, blast

en: men, hen, pen, ten, went, sent, dent, bend, send, tent

est: west, best, quest, guest, nest, rest, vest, pest, crest

ig: big, jig, fig, pig, wig, dig, rig, twig, swig, piglet

ill: fill, bill, grill, will, pill, dill, drill, gill, hill, still, millet

ock: rock, lock, sock, block, clock, dock, pocket, rocket, socket

og: hog, log, bog, dog, frog, fog, jog, smog, slog

un: sun, run, nun, bun, gun, fun, pun, junk, trunk, skunk

uck: truck, tuck, muck, ruckus, puck, duck, buck, luck, yuck, bucket

Book 4

qu: quill, quack, quip, quick, quit, quilt, quiz

st: stop, step, stamp, stuck, stiff, stack, fist, mist, list, stump, stem

dr: drip, drop, drum, drug, dress, drill, drift, drink, drab

ck: lock, pack, duck, rock, wick, deck, clock, luck, quack, track

mp: camp, stamp, damp, limp, pump, lump, stump, lamp, bump

tr: trip, trot, trap, trust, trim, trunk, track, trick, trumpet, tramp

❧ 24 ❧

SHORT VOWEL:

WORD FOLD-UPS

Similar to the preceding activity, Word Fold-Ups give your child additional reading practice. The material's bright, varied colors help keep interest high. Use familiar words and add new ones to expand her vocabulary.

☞ **What You Need:**

Construction paper, ruler, scissors, colored markers, basket

✄ **To Prepare:**

1. Cut a 1¾- by 12-inch strip of colored construction paper.

2. Choose a word list from the following page. At the top of the strip, write and underline the letters common to that list.

3. Fold up the bottom edge of the strip so it rests just below the underlined letters. Press the fold.

4. Open the paper and write the word list under the top letters. When you close the Fold-Up, the words are hidden, so only the underlined letters at the top show.

5. Make more Fold-Ups, using assorted colors of construction paper. Place them in a basket.

Examples:

Here are six word lists to get you started. Make more Word Fold-Ups using lists from the previous lesson, Short Vowel: Words I Can Read (page 108) or from Short Vowel Words (page 93):

ot: pot, hot, dot, lot, slot, got, trot, plot, blot

sl: slam, slot, slip, slap, slept, sled, slacks, slump, slop

cr: crib, crab, crop, crisp, crust, crack, cramp, crest, cross

ust: crust, must, dust, rust, trust, just, gust

gr: grin, grand, grill, grip, grunt, grasp, grab, grant, grit, granddad

um: plum, drum, sum, stump, grump, lump, hum, jump, plump

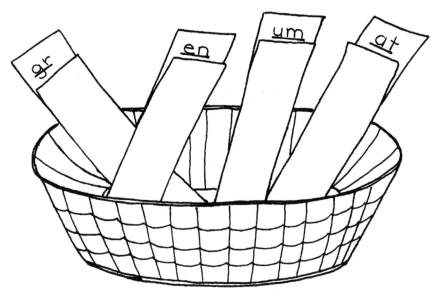

☆ **Activity:**

Invite your child to take the Word Fold-Ups out one at a time and read them. Make the opening of each one mysterious as you say, "Shall we open it and see what's inside?"

Variation:

For writing practice, invite her to make Word Fold-Ups of her own, using colored markers or colored paper for variety.

❧ 25 ❧

SHORT VOWEL:

TEAM BOOKS

Read, write, cut, glue, and color! This project gives your child practice writing short vowel words as he makes five Team Books—one for each vowel. Part of their appeal is that he gets to help create them!

☞ What You Need:

Paper or cardstock, construction paper, large writing paper (page 36), soft-lead colored pencils, scissors, pen, glue, Short Vowel Pictures–small (page 36), hole punch, yarn

✄ To Prepare:

1. To make the pages for each Team Book, cut three 8½- by 11-inch sheets of paper into quarters. You will use ten of these quarter-sheet pieces.

2. Draw or glue ten different *a* Short Vowel Pictures onto the ten pages, one per sheet. Place each image on the upper part of its page, leaving the bottom blank.

3. Repeat steps 1 and 2 to make *e, i, o,* and *u* Team Books pages.

☆ **Activity:**

Do this project all at once or over several days. Let your child's interest guide the speed of the work.

1. Give your child the Team Book pages in sets. Ask him to look at a picture and say its name. Have him write it on lined paper, using red pencil for consonants and blue pencil for vowels. Instruct him to cut the word out and glue it under the picture on the Team Book page.

2. Suggest he color the picture.

3. When ten pages of the Team Book are completed, cut a construction paper cover, punch the pages, and bind them with yarn. Write "Allen's (child's name) *a* (or *e, i, o, u)* Team Book" on the cover. Invite him to decorate it creatively.

4. On another day, give him a different set of Team Book pages. Encourage him to complete one book for each vowel.

5. Read the books together and add them to his library.

❧ 26 ❧

SHORT VOWEL:

PHRASE BOOKS

As soon as your child learns to decipher short vowel words, give her lots of opportunities to practice her new skill. Phrase Books use only short vowel words, so she can sound them out easily and experience the thrill of reading.

☞ What You Need:

Paper or cardstock, scissors, colored pencils or markers, glue, Short Vowel Pictures (page 36), hole punch, yarn

✄ To Prepare:

1. Cut paper or cardstock into rectangles for pages. Punch holes along one side and bind with yarn.

2. On the inside front cover and on all left-hand pages, glue on a Short Vowel Picture such as *nut, hen,* or *pig.* Or draw the images, if you prefer.

3. On the blank right-hand pages, write short vowel phrases to match the pictures.

4. Write your child's name on the cover and invite her to decorate it.

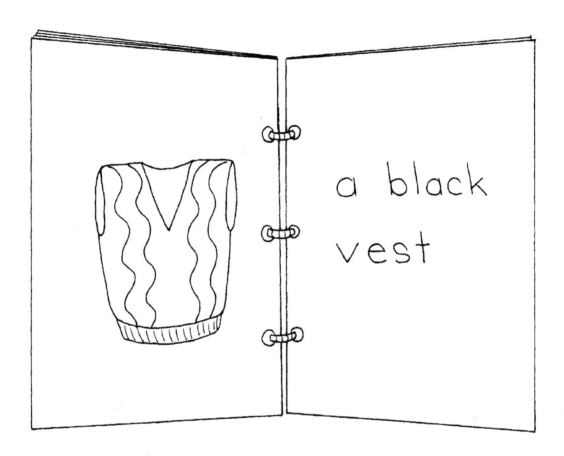

☆ **Activity:**

1. Tell your child that when *a* is used by itself in a sentence, it says *u*. Then invite her to read the book and color the pictures. Congratulate her on reading her first book!

2. Add the Phrase Book to her library. Encourage her to read it to friends and family members. Make sure she knows how proud you are of her efforts.

Examples:

Here are ideas for three Phrase Books.

Book 1	**Book 2**	**Book 3**
a wet frog	a black vest	Mom has red lipstick
a soft cat	a dog can wag	a big bell
a big jet	a fun pup	kitten and jam
a pink pig	rust on a van	a hen pecks
ten red pens	snap a twig	button a jacket
Tom can grin	a cat can hiss	pet a dog
pack a bag	a lit wick	a duck on a pond
a drill on a rug	mint gum	Kim smells a plant

SMALL LETTER CARDS

Now that your child has learned the letter sounds and built words with Letter Cards (page 62), it's time to introduce a set of smaller cards (with duplicate letters). Small Letter Cards—used for forming words and sentences—serve as an easily stored movable alphabet for the rest of this book.

☞ **What You Need:**

White cardstock, ruler, scissors, red and blue markers. To store the Small Letter Cards, you will need either three egg cartons or two eighteen compartment plastic boxes, such as those used for embroidery thread, beads, or fishing tackle.

✂ **To Prepare:**

1. Cut cardstock into 170 1¼- by 1½-inch rectangles. This gives you enough cards to make four of each letter and punctuation mark, one capital for each letter, and have a few extras.

2. Write the consonants *(b, c, d, f, g, h, j, k, l, m, n, p, q, r, s, t, v, w, x, y, z)* with red marker. Make four cards for each lower case letter and one for each capital. Place the finished Small Letter Cards in the egg cartons or boxes, working from left to right in alphabetical order and leaving spaces for the vowels.

3. Write the vowels *(a, e, i, o, u)* with blue marker. Make four cards for each small letter and one card for each capital. Add the finished cards to the egg cartons or boxes.

4. On the remaining blank cards, write four each of these punctuation
symbols: period (.), comma (,), question mark (?), exclamation point (!),
semicolon (;), colon (:), dash (-), en dash (–), em dash (—), and quotation
mark (" ") —write one quotation mark on each of four cards to make two
sets. Place the punctuation mark cards in the final spaces in the third egg
carton or second box, after *z*. Each of these symbols is discussed in Punctuation Guide (page 324). Your child doesn't need to know what they all
mean now, but they will be available when he needs them.

☆ **Activity:**

Show your child the Small Letter Cards and say the letter sounds together.
Play a little game where you call out a letter sound and he finds the correct
Small Letter Card. If he has trouble making the transition to the smaller
cards, set out the original set of larger Letter Cards (page 62) and have him
match a Small Letter Card to each big one. He will use the Small Letter
Cards in all future activities that require a moveable alphabet.

✥ 28 ✥

HELPING WORDS 1

Words like the, she, *and* of *don't follow the short vowel pattern your child has learned, but they are necessary for reading and writing short sentences. This lesson takes the mystery and frustration out of seeing these words and trying to "sound them out." They will, instead, be friends she is familiar with.*

Note: The ten Helping Words given in this lesson are all that are needed to do the activities in Part 2. Part 3 begins with Helping Words 2, which introduces additional non-phonetic words.

☞ **What You Need:**

Small Letter Cards (page 118), large writing paper (page 36), red and blue soft-lead colored pencils, construction paper, scissors, hole punch, yarn

✂ **To Prepare:**

Cut sheets of writing paper in half to make smaller writing pages.

☆ **Activity 1: Building Helping Words**

1. Bring the Small Letter Cards to a table. Set out the letters for one of the Helping Words (listed on the next page).

2. Tell your child the word, and then use it in a sentence. For example, *"The. The ducks can swim."*

3. Scramble the letters and invite her to build the word.

4. Ask her to use the word in a sentence of her own.

Example: Ten Helping Words

- a
- I
- is
- of
- we
- to
- he
- she
- has
- the

☆ **Activity 2: Writing Helping Words**

1. Say a Helping Word and ask your child to form it with the letter cards.

2. Place a half sheet of writing paper next to the word.

3. Write the word once on the top line of the page. Use red pencil for the consonants and blue for the vowels. Have her copy the word three times beneath.

Invite your child to complete several Helping Words pages each day. Once all ten pages are done, form them into a book. Cut a construction paper cover, punch three holes down the side, and bind with yarn—or simply staple down the side. Write "Helping Words" on the cover. Encourage her to read you the book often.

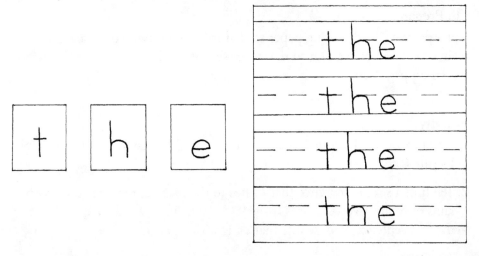

❧ 29 ❧

SHORT VOWEL:

BUILD & WRITE SENTENCES

Now that your child can read and write short vowel words and has learned a few Helping Words, he is ready to link them together into proper sentences that begin with capital letters and end with a period, question mark, or exclamation point. (See Punctuation Guide, page 324.) Encourage him to do one or more pages daily until he has made several books and the work is easy.

☞ **What You Need:**

Large writing paper (page 36), Small Letter Cards (page 118), Short Vowel Picture Cards (page 91) or other short vowel pictures, soft-lead colored pencils, plain or colored paper, construction paper, scissors, glue, hole punch, yarn

✄ **To Prepare:**

Cut a piece of lined writing paper so that it fits lengthwise onto a sheet of plain or colored paper, and so that three sets of writing lines are available, as shown on page 124.

☆ **Activity:**

1. Set out the Small Letter Cards. Invite your child to choose a Short Vowel Picture Card.

2. Tell him a simple sentence that relates to the picture, making sure it contains only short vowel words (page 93) and helping words (page 120). For the first sentence, choose one that ends with a period.

Examples:

- Picture: hat
  Sentence: Sam has a hat.

- Picture: fig
  Sentence: The fig is big.

- Picture: can
  Sentence: The can is in a bag.

- Picture: log
  Sentence: Meg fit a peg in the log.

- Picture: cup
  Sentence: The cup of milk is hot.

- Picture: camel
  Sentence: The camel has a big hump!

- Picture: pig
  Sentence: It is a pink pig.

- Picture: stamp
  Sentence: Will Pam lick the stamp?

- Picture: pup
  Sentence: Mom and Dad hug the pup.

- Picture: tent or dog
  Sentence: The wet dog ran in the tent.

- Picture: prize ribbon
  Sentence: Will he win the red ribbon?

- Picture: bug or net
  Sentence: Dan has a bug in his net!

- Picture: top
  Sentence: The red top spins fast.

- Picture: nest
  Sentence: A hen sits on the nest.

- Picture: fox or box
  Sentence: Can the fox jump in the box?

- Picture: cat or bed
  Sentence: A cat naps on the soft bed.

- Picture: bug or nut
  Sentence: The bug hid in the nut.

- Picture: trumpet
  Sentence: Tess and Nick got trumpets!

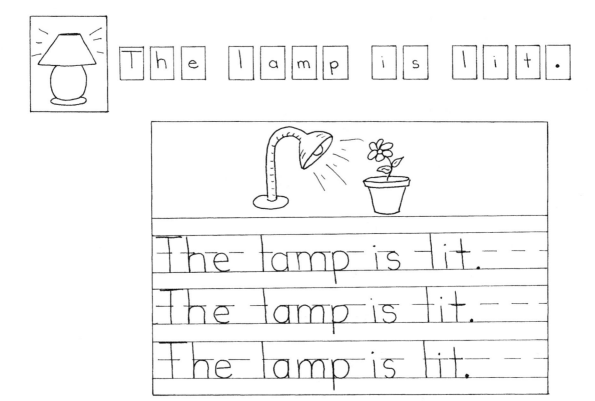

3. Ask him to use the Small Letter Cards to build the words, in order, from left to right. Show him how to start the sentence with a capital letter. Explain that all sentences begin with capital letters. Also explain that personal names—such as Meg, Tom, and Pam—begin with capital letters.

4. Show him how to end the sentence with a period. Explain that a period means *stop* and shows that the sentence has ended. Have him read the sentence aloud.

5. Using red pencil for consonants and blue pencil for vowels, print the sentence on the top line of the prepared writing paper. Ask him to read it aloud. Again point out that it begins with a capital letter and ends with a period.

6. Have him write the sentence two more times on the lines beneath.

7. Show him how to apply glue to the edge of the writing paper and press it onto a piece of plain or colored paper, leaving a space at the top. Suggest he decorate the blank area with a drawing to illustrate the sentence.

8. Explain that question marks are used at the end of sentences that ask questions and that exclamation marks are used to show excitement or strong emotion. Write a period, question mark, and exclamation mark on a fresh piece of lined paper and have him practice writing them.

9. Invite him to choose another Short Vowel Picture Card and repeat steps 2–7. Help where needed, such as by pointing out words containing two letters that say the same sounds, such as *will* and *lick*.

10. Save the pages and display your child's best work on a wall or bulletin board. When ten pages are done, add a construction paper cover, punch holes down the side, and bind with yarn. Write "(child's name) Sentence Book" on the cover and invite him to decorate it. Add the book to his library.

❧ 30 ❧

SHORT VOWEL:

SENTENCE JUMBLES

This lesson offers more practice reading and building sentences. It also encourages logical thinking as your child puts the words in order.

☞ **What You Need:**

Large writing paper (page 36), lead or colored pencils, construction paper, scissors, glue, rubber bands, basket or box

✂ **To Prepare:**

1. With lead or colored pencil, print a short vowel sentence on a strip of writing paper (see Short Vowel Words, page 93, and Helping Words 1, page 120, for ideas). Begin the sentence with a capital letter and end it with a period, question mark, or exclamation point.

2. Glue the sentence onto a strip of colored construction paper that is a bit larger than the writing paper. Let dry.

3. Divide the sentence by cutting between the words. Cut off extra construction paper on the right and left edges. Leave a border along the top and bottom edges.

4. Secure the Sentence Jumbles pieces with a rubber band and place them in a basket or box.

5. Repeat steps 1–4 to make more Sentence Jumbles.

☆ **Activity:**

1. Invite your child to put one Sentence Jumble on a table or rug, placing the words at random.

2. Ask her to read each word. When she finds the first word of the sentence, have her set it to the left, continuing until the sentence is complete.

3. Have her read it aloud. Remind her that sentences begin with capital letters and end with either a period, question mark, or exclamation point.

4. Demonstrate how to stack and secure the word pieces with a rubber band to put them away. Encourage her to choose another Sentence Jumble and build it herself.

31

Short Vowel:

Sentence Books

Reading these simple homemade books filled with words your child is familiar with helps build his confidence.

☞ **What You Need:**

Paper or cardstock, Short Vowel Pictures—large (page 36) (or pictures or stickers depicting short vowel words), scissors, glue, colored markers, hole punch, yarn

✄ **To Prepare:**

1. Cut paper or cardstock into rectangular pages. Punch holes down one side of the pages and bind with yarn.

2. Choose Short Vowel Pictures, stickers, or other images of things that have short vowel names.

3. Decide if you want the pictures to tell a simple story. If so, arrange them in the desired order. Glue them onto the left hand pages.

4. On the right pages, use colored markers to write short, easy-to-read, descriptive sentences to accompany the images (see Short Vowel Words, page 93, and Helping Words 1, page 120, for word lists).

5. Choose a title for the book and write it on the cover.

Examples:

The pictures go on the left pages, the sentences on the right pages.

- Picture: fan
  Sentence: Jan has a pink fan.

- Picture: clock
  Sentence: A clock is on the desk.

- Picture: bathtub mat
  Sentence: A tub mat will help us not to slip.

- Picture: hat
  Sentence: The hat has lots of red ribbon on it.

- Picture: stacked cups
  Sentence: Can Mat stack the cups?

- Picture: stamps
  Sentence: Get me a stamp!

- Picture: skunk
  Sentence: Tim has a skunk!

- Picture: kitten on a rug
  Sentence: The kitten sits on a red rug.

- Picture: rabbit
  Sentences: The rabbit has a grin. It will hop to a bin of carrots to get a snack.

- Picture: nesting hen
  Sentences: Pet the hen. Get the eggs from the nest. Set the eggs in the pink basket.

☆ **Activity:**

Encourage your child to read you the books often and suggest he read them to his friends.

32

WRITING SMALLER

Once your child has had lots of practice using large ⅞-inch-rule paper, it is time to introduce smaller ⅝-inch-rule writing paper. This activity is the next step in the development of her writing skills. It lets you review how she is forming the letters, and gives her a chance to focus on letter formation and adjust her style to fit within the smaller spaces of the new paper.

This is an ongoing project, so plan to have your child do several pages each day. An Alphabet Sticker Chart provides incentive. This size writing paper will be used for many of the following activities, until she is comfortable using notebook paper—first wide-rule, then college-rule.

☞ **What You Need:**

Small writing paper (page 36), soft-lead colored pencils, lead pencil, construction paper, envelope, assorted stickers, ruler, scissors, stapler

✀ **To Prepare:**

1. Cut the writing paper into twenty-six 2- by 4½-inch pieces, so that two sets of writing lines are included, as shown on the next page. Put the strips in an envelope.

2. Make an Alphabet Sticker Chart, as illustrated on page 133, to help your child track her progress. Mount the chart on a wall near her work area.

☆ **Activity:**

1. Compliment your child on all the good writing she has done. Explain that it is time for her to take the next step by using paper with lines placed closer together. She will form the letters the same way, but must print smaller to make them fit between the lines.

2. Give her a prepared paper and write *a* on it with a colored pencil. Have her copy four more *a*'s on the line.

3. Ask her to write five *a*'s with lead pencil on the second line.

4. Congratulate her on her work and ask her to place a sticker next to the *a* on the Alphabet Sticker Chart.

5. Encourage her to do the *b* page. Write the first letter for her, then let her complete the page as before. Suggest she use different colored pencils on the top lines of each page and lead pencil on the bottom ones.

6. When all the pages are completed, help her arrange them alphabetically into two books titled "a–m" and "n–z". Add construction paper covers and staple at the sides.

7. If desired, make another set of books with capital letters.

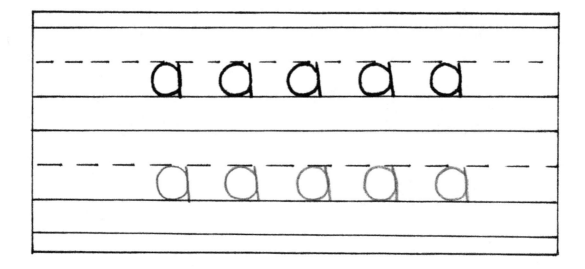

Alphabet Sticker Chart

a	b	c	d
e	f	g	h
i	j	k	l
m	n	o	p
q	r	s	t
u	v	w	x
y	z		

❧ 33 ❧

SHORT VOWEL:

CUT & COLOR BOOKS

Cut, color, glue, and write! This activity combines reading and writing into a hands-on project that will satisfy even the most fidgety child.

☞ **What You Need:**

Plain white paper, cardstock, Short Vowel Pictures–large (page 36), scissors, ruler, colored pencils or markers, pen, glue, hole punch, yarn

✂ **To Prepare:**

1. Choose ten Short Vowel Pictures for each book you plan to make. Cut them out along the guide lines and set them aside.

2. Cut two 5- by 6-inch pieces of cardstock for the front and back covers.

3. Cut sheets of white paper to make nine pages for the book. Punch three holes along one edge of the pages and covers, then bind them with yarn.

4. At the top of each right hand page, write a word that matches one of the ten Short Vowel Pictures you chose. Beneath it, print a sentence that uses the word, drawing from Short Vowel Words (page 93) and Helping Words 1 (page 120). Below the sentence, draw a line for your child to copy the word on. Write the last word and sentence on the inside back cover. The inside front cover and all the left pages should be blank; the right pages should have the writing.

☆ **Activity:**

1. Give your child the ten Short Vowel Pictures and the book. Have him say the word at the top of a page, read the sentence, then write the word on the line. Have him find and color the matching picture, then cut around and glue it onto the left-hand page.

2. When the Cut-and-Color book is complete, read it together and add it to his library. Encourage him to read it to himself, as well as to friends and family members.

Variation:

Increase the difficulty for older children by increasing the number of pages and/or making the text longer. Ask them to copy sentences instead of words and have them draw their own pictures.

༈ 34 ༈

Short Vowel:

Action Stickers

Action Stickers provide additional reading practice. They give your child a little reward for completing a task and a quick break from seated work to "get the jiggles out."

☞ **What You Need:**

Large blank stickers, pen

✂ **To Prepare:**

1. Write short directions on the stickers, using Short Vowel Words (page 93) and Helping Words 1 (page 120). Here are some ideas:

- Smell the jam.

- Get a map.

- Hop and skip.

- Sip a cup of milk.

- Pick up the cat.

- Jump on the mat.

- Hug Mom and Dad.

- Zip up the jacket.

- Set a black pen on the desk.

- Fit ten nuts in a cup.

- Get the red blanket.

- Sit on the bed.

- Jump on the rug.

- Set the mittens on the desk.

- Fill a glass.

- Dust the plant.

- Get a hat.

- Get Dad a snack.

- Hand Mom a stamp.

- Hop on the rug.

2. Place the stickers in a pretty bowl, basket, or box.

☆ **Activity:**

Action Stickers are great little rewards. Invite your child to choose a sticker, read it, do the indicated action, and then put it on a completed work page or other fun place.

✥ 35 ✥

READING CHARTS

Use these charts to help your child track his progress, give him a sense of accomplishment, and encourage further reading.

☞ What You Need:

Construction paper, colored markers, stickers, books to read

✂ To Prepare:

1. Draw lines on a sheet of construction paper, as illustrated on the next page. Make space for stickers on the right side.

2. Write the names of homemade and library books on the lines. Keep the list long enough to challenge your child, but not so long as to overwhelm him. When one chart is finished, make another. Begin with simple (even one-word and one-sentence) books and progress to full-length ones as his reading skills improve.

3. Attach the Reading Chart to a bulletin board or wall. Place a basket of assorted stickers nearby.

☆ Activity:

1. Ask your child to read the first book on the chart.

2. When he finishes it, invite him to put a sticker next to the name of the book.

3. Celebrate each time he completes a chart!

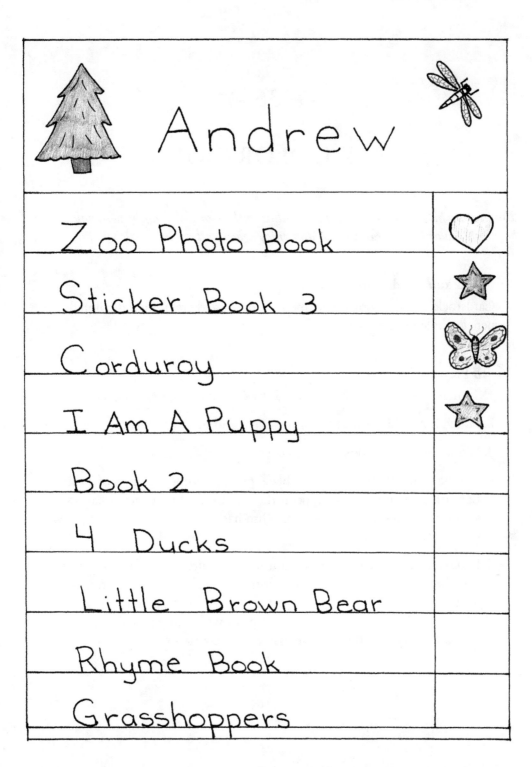

Andrew

Zoo Photo Book	♡
Sticker Book 3	★
Corduroy	🦋
I Am A Puppy	★
Book 2	
4 Ducks	
Little Brown Bear	
Rhyme Book	
Grasshoppers	

∂ 36 ∂

My Color Book

This activity helps your child become familiar with color words as she personalizes her book. My Color Book is fun to read and enjoy again and again.

☞ **What You Need:**

Cardstock, ruler, scissors, black pen, colored markers, lead and colored pencils, hole punch, yarn

✄ **To Prepare:**

1. To make the book pages, cut ten 5- by 6-inch pieces of cardstock.

2. Punch holes along one edge of the pages and bind with yarn.

3. Write "My Color Book" on the cover.

4. On the inside front cover, use a black pen to outline a picture of a mitten. Beneath it, with red marker, print the word *red*. On the facing page write a corresponding sentence, such as, "Jim has a ___ mitten." Your child will write *red* on the line.

5. Repeat for the remaining pages, outlining pictures with black pen on the left, then, with matching marker, writing the color word beneath and a related sentence on the right page. For "white" use lead pencil or glue a dark colored paper over the page and print with white pencil or crayon. The last sentence will be on the inside back cover.

Examples:

- red: Jim has a ___ mitten.

- orange: The _____ pumpkin fits in a big box.

- yellow: The cat has a _____ rug.

- green: Tom cuts the _____ grass.

- blue: Erin has a ____ fan.

- purple: She drinks from the _____ glass.

- brown: The frog sits on a _____ log.

- white: Fran is on a _____ blanket.

- black: It is a fast _____ truck.

brown

The frog sits on a ____ log.

☆ **Activity:**

1. Give your child the book and explain that each page is a little project.

2. Invite her to color the first picture and read the color word. Have her trace over the color word with matching colored pencil, then write the word on the line on the facing page.

3. Once he has written the color word, have him read the entire sentence aloud.

4. When the book is completed, read it together and add it to his library. Encourage him to read it to friends.

Variation:

Make a second book with other colors, such as pink, peach, teal, violet, gold, silver, and grey.

❧ 37 ❧

STICKER BOOKS

This engaging project encourages your child to read and count. He also learns about shapes and reviews color words as he creates books that are uniquely his own.

☞ **What You Need:**

Plain paper or cardstock, colored cardstock, scissors, ruler, colored markers, stickers such as colored dots and stars, hole punch, yarn

✂ **To Prepare:**

1. Cut paper or cardstock into 5- by 6-inch pages. Choose several colors of dots, stars, or other stickers to use with the book.

2. Give the book a colorful cardstock cover. Title it "My Dots and Stars Book" (or other name that refers to the stickers you are using) and decorate it with stickers. Punch holes along the sides of the cover and pages, then bind with yarn.

3. Using different colored markers, outline a simple picture of a Short Vowel Word (page 93) on each left-hand page.

4. On the blank page opposite each picture, write with colored marker directions for putting certain numbers, types, and colors of stickers inside each outline.

Examples:

The pictures go on the left pages, the sentences on the right pages.

- Picture: sun
  Sentences: The sun is hot. Stick 7 gold stars on it.

- Picture: hat
  Sentences: The hat has a brim. It has 3 green dots and 4 silver dots on it.

- Picture: dress
  Sentences: Kim has dots on a dress. It has 10 red dots, 10 blue dots, and 1 green dot.

- Picture: hat
  Sentences: A hat is a lot of fun! The hat has 4 blue stars and 2 green stars. It has 1 blue dot on the pocket.

- Picture: carrot
  Sentences: The carrot has 2 gold stars and 5 gold dots on it. Gus hands the carrot to his rabbit.

- Picture: box
  Sentences: The box is a gift. It has 3 silver stars on the ribbon and 6 red dots on the box.

- Picture: glass
  Sentences: Jill has a glass of milk. Press 2 blue dots, 2 yellow dots, and 2 green dots on it.

- Picture: drum
  Sentences: Mack smacks the drum. Fran taps the drum. Stick 5 gold stars and 1 silver star on the drum.

- Picture: hill
  Sentences: Quick! Stick 10 orange dots on the hill.

- Picture: two cups
  Sentences: Ann's cup has 6 yellow stars on it. Fred's cup has 6 blue stars on it.

- Picture: bug
  Sentences: The bug has 8 black dots on it.

☆ **Activity:**

1. Give your child the stickers and the book. Introduce him to any words that don't follow the short vowel pattern, such as *stars*.

2. Invite him to read the directions for each picture, then apply the correct number, type, and color of stickers.

3. When he finishes, read the book together and add it to his library. Every time he reads the book, have him count the stickers.

PART 3

PARTNER WORDS

Letters in English often have different sounds, depending on which other letters they are paired with. Fortunately, most of these changes follow rules. This section presents these rules, along with new words that expand your child's vocabulary and reading ability tremendously.

The activities in Part 3 introduce letter partners. The name *partners* refers to sets of letters that combine to make new sounds: for example, the letters *s* and *h* make *sh,* as in the word *ship*. Likewise, the letter *a* says its long vowel sound when teamed with *e* in *cake* or *i* in *rain*. To highlight similarities, groups of related words are presented in sets.

Continuing the pattern of creating books, these new words are written—singly and in sentences—and gathered into booklets. Working through these projects gives your child the tools to read most English words, including those far beyond his grade level. This is a good opportunity to teach him how to use a dictionary to look up definitions and check spelling.

Even if you know little about language, with this guide you can teach with confidence. Just relax, follow the directions, and watch your child bloom.

✌ 38 ✌

HELPING WORDS 2

This lesson teaches your child a second set of non-phonetic words, which will enable her to read longer, more interesting stories. Use this activity to introduce additional non-phonetic words that you note she will encounter in reading material.

☞ What You Need:

Small Letter Cards (page 118), small writing paper (page 36), red and blue soft-lead writing pencils, construction paper, scissors, hole punch, yarn

✀ To Prepare:

Cut sheets of writing paper in half.

☆ Activity 1: Building Helping Words

1. Bring the Small Letter Cards to a table. Set out the letters for a new Helping Word.

2. Tell your child the name of the word, for example, *are*. Use it in a sentence, such as, "We *are* having potatoes for dinner."

3. Scramble the letters and ask her to rebuild it.

4. Invite her to say the word in a sentence of her own.

Example: More Helping Words

Set 1	Set 2
no	have
go	this
are	look
out	here
put	they
see	were
with	said
do	please

☆ **Activity 2: Writing Helping Words**

1. Ask your child to build a Helping Word with the Small Letter Cards.

2. Place a half sheet of writing paper next to the word.

3. Write the word once for her on the top line of the page, using red pencil for the consonants and blue for the vowels. Have her print the word three times on the lines below.

Encourage her to write several Helping Words pages each day until she has completed both sets. Form the pages into two booklets. Cut a construction paper cover for each one, then punch three holes down the side and bind with yarn. Or simply staple down the left side. Write "More Helping Words" on the covers. Have her read you the books often, until the words are no longer a challenge.

ᔟ 39 ᔟ

PARTNERS:

WORD BOOKLETS

We begin partner work by introducing sh, ch, th, *and* wh *in Word Booklets. Knowing these will enable your child to read many new words.*

☞ What You Need:

Small Letter Cards (page 118), small writing paper (page 36), construction paper, scissors, soft-lead colored pencils, lead pencil, stapler

✄ To Prepare:

To make the Word Booklets pages, cut writing paper into strips that are one set of writing lines wide and 4½-inches long.

☆ Activity:

Tell your child that he is going to learn lots of new words, called Partner Words, and that *partners* are what we call two or more letters that team up to make a new sound. Explain that he is going to make four booklets with Partner Words.

1. Set out the Small Letter Cards *s* and *h*. Place them together and explain that they are "letter partners." Say the *sh* sound. Have him repeat it.

2. Write a list of *sh* words on a piece of writing paper. Ask him to read the words.

3. Instruct him to copy one word onto each strip of prepared writing paper, printing the letter partners *sh* with colored pencil and the remaining letters with lead pencil.

4. When all the words are written, collect the pages and cut a construction paper cover. Write *sh* on the cover and staple at the side.

5. Add the book to his library and encourage him to read it often.

6. Repeat Activity 1–5 with the letter partners *ch, th,* and *wh.*

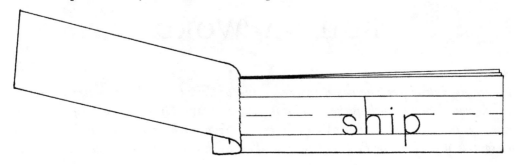

Examples:

<u>**sh**</u>	<u>**ch**</u>	<u>**th**</u>	<u>**wh**</u>
ship	chip	thank	whip
shop	chin	thin	when
shut	channel	think	what
shift	chill	thunder	where
shin	lunch	this	whisker
wish	crunch	that	whisper
lash	finch	them	whack
dish	much	there	whisk
fish	bunch	then	which

Notice that *th* makes two different sounds; in the last five words it makes more of a buzzing sound.

PARTNERS: LONG VOWEL

BUILD-A-WORD

This activity introduces long vowel partners—two or three letters that together make the long vowel sounds, such as the a sound in c<u>a</u>k<u>e</u> and r<u>ai</u>n. Over the course of this project, your child creates a Long Vowel Partner Book for each set of letters and for the two sounds of y. Make the Balloon Chart, as illustrated, so she can track her progress.

☞ **What You Need:**

Red, green, yellow, blue, and orange construction or printer paper; small writing paper (page 36), scissors, ruler, pen, soft-lead colored pencils, stapler, Partners Pictures (page 36), Small Letter Cards (page 118) glue, tape, basket, yarn (optional)

✁ **To Prepare:**

Build the Balloon Chart on a wall, bulletin board, or piece of poster board, as shown on the next page.

1. Assemble the clown from colorful construction paper. Make the strings from yarn or paper.

2. Cut sets of balloons (four each of red, green, yellow, and blue; and three of orange). Write these letter partners on the balloons:

> red: a–e, ai, ay, eigh   blue: o–e, oe, oa, ow
> green: ee, ea, ey, y   orange: u–e, ue, ew
> yellow: i–e, ie, igh, y

Set these aside in a basket or envelope. Your child will tape these on the chart as she finishes each Long Vowel Partner Book.

3. On the Balloon Chart, outline—with matching colored marker—where the construction paper balloons will be placed.

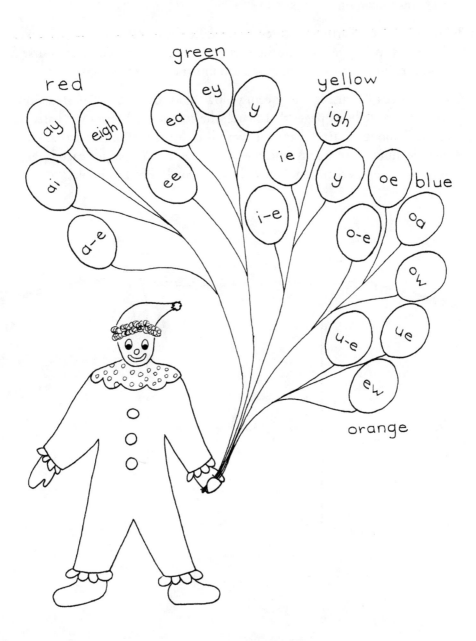

✂ To Prepare: Long Vowel Partner Book Pages

1. For the first book, *a–e*, cut red paper into ten 4¼- by 5½-inch pages. Staple them at the side and write *a–e* on the cover.

2. Cut ten 3- by 4½- inch pieces of writing paper to fit on the colored paper pages, as shown on the next page.

3. Prepare ten *a–e* Partner Pictures to illustrate the *a–e* Partner Words. To do this, either print and cut out the Partner Pictures or sketch them yourself. If your child is artistic, he may wish to illustrate his own book.

4. Repeat steps 1–3 using red, green, yellow, blue, and orange construction paper to create book pages that match the colors and long vowel partners on the Balloon Chart. Check the word lists at the end of this activity to find the number of words, and therefore pages, you need for each book, as some have less than ten. You will have a total of fifteen books.

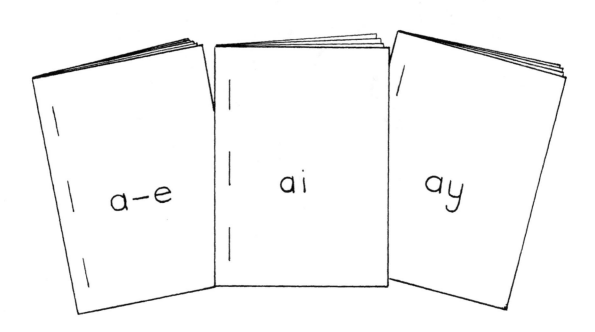

☆ **Activity:**

1. Show your child a Partner Picture, for example, *cake.* Say it's name. Explain that the *a* and *e* are partners. Together, they make the *a* say its long sound.

2. Use the Small Letter Cards to build the word *cake* for her. Discuss the meaning of the word if it is unfamiliar. Use it in a sentence.

3. Bring out a prepared writing paper. Write *a–e* at the top of the page and *cake* on the next line, using a colored pencil to form the long-vowel partners *a–e* and a lead pencil to form the consonants.

4. Ask her to copy *cake* three times on the lines below. Encourage her to say the word each time she writes it.

5. Have her glue the paper onto the first right-hand page of the book. Then invite her to color and glue the matching picture onto the inside front cover.

6. This is an ongoing project, so encourage her to write a few pages each day. When the book is completed, congratulate her and invite her to tape the first balloon to the Balloon Chart.

7. Introduce the next set of Partner Pictures, *ai,* and repeat steps 1–6. Continue in like manner until the Balloon Chart is completed. When you get to the letter *y,* explain that although it has no partner, it is included in this exercise because it makes more than one sound.

Long Vowel Partner Words

Long Vowel *a* Partner Words

a–e: cake, cane, gate, drape, scale, game, rake, skate, vase, plane

ai: nail, snail, paint, train, rain, pail, grain, waist, quail, mail

ay: ray, pay, clay, hay, gray, crayon, play, tray, bay, stay

eigh: eight, sleigh, weigh, neigh, neighbor

Long Vowel *e* Partner Words

ee: bee, seed, eel, wheel, green, tree, beet, week, queen, heel

ea: sea, pea, leaf, read, peach, team, peak, leak, seal, seat

ey: key, monkey, honey, chimney, turkey, donkey, valley, barley, jockey, trolley

y: candy, lady, sixty, fairy, jelly, daisy, penny, dolly, funny, happy

Long Vowel *i* Partner Words

i–e: smile, dive, pine, kite, nine, five, tire, slide, hive, lime

ie: pie, lie, die, cried, fried, tried, tie, spies, flies, dries

igh: light, high, sigh, might, bright, night, fight, tight, right, delight

y: sky, my, cry, shy, multiply, dry, python, fry, dragonfly, bicycle

Long Vowel *o* Partner Words

o–e: rose, robe, bone, nose, store, hose, stove, smoke, cone, note

oe: doe, foe, toe, woe, hoe, goes, tomatoes, potatoes

oa: boat, coat, goat, road, croak, soap, toast, foal, cloak, throat

ow: mow, crow, bowl, window, snow, yellow, pillow, arrow, elbow, throw

Long Vowel *u* Partner Words

u–e: mule, duke, cube, cute, dilute, tube, tune, mute, lute, flute

ue: hue, due, cue, argue, fuel, duel, value, continue, clue, true

ew: mew, view, pewter, new, few, stew, blew, drew, chew, crew

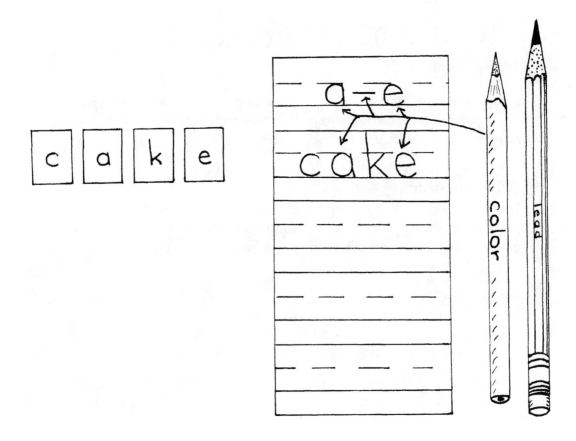

❧ 41 ❧

PARTNERS: LONG VOWEL

TEAM BOOKS

Team Books give your child additional practice writing the long vowel partner words and help expand his vocabulary. The word team *refers to sets of words that share the same partners, such as* seed, tree, beet, *and* queen.

☞ **What You Need:**

Partner Pictures (page 36), Long Vowel Partner Words (page 156), plain paper, small writing paper (page 36), construction paper, scissors, ruler, pen, glue, lead and colored pencils, staples, yarn (optional)

✁ **To Prepare:**

Make one Team Book for each long vowel partner.

1. To make a Team Book, cut plain paper into quarters to make ten pages.

2. Beginning with the *a–e* book, glue an *a–e* Partner Picture onto the upper part of each page, leaving the bottom blank. Complete all ten pages in this manner.

3. Repeat steps 1 and 2 to make other long vowel Team Books.

☆ **Activity:**

Do a few pages at a time, letting your child's interest guide the speed of the work.

1. Give your child a set of prepared Team Book pages. Ask him to look at a picture, say its name, and then write it on lined paper. Once this is done, have him cut out the word and glue it under the picture on the Team Book page. Invite him to color the illustration.

2. When all ten pages of the Team Book are finished, cut a construction paper cover, punch holes in the pages, and bind them with yarn; or simply staple at the side. Write "(child's name) *a–e* Team Book" on the front. Invite him to decorate it creatively.

3. Another day, give him a new set of Team Book pages. Encourage him to complete a Team Book for each of the long-vowel partners.

4. Read the books together and add them to his library.

ॐ 42 ॐ

PARTNERS:

FILL‑IN‑THE‑BLANK BOOKS

These handcrafted books give young students a fun way to practice reading and writing. They also introduce new words to increase vocabulary. Try making them on subjects that appeal to your child, such as favorite movie characters, dogs, trucks, gymnastics, basketball, or cooking. Or use them to introduce a new topic, such as musical instruments or birds.

Note: For younger children, make Fill-in-the-Blank Books with Short Vowel Words (page 93). For older students, write paragraphs—replacing key words with lines—that focus on history, science, or other topics.

☞ **What You Need:**

Paper, scissors, pen, hole punch, yarn

✄ **To Prepare:**

1. Decide on the size of your book, then cut paper into rectangles for pages. Punch holes along one side and bind with yarn.

2. Invent or find a short story to copy, then write it on the pages of your book. For beginning readers, write one sentence per page, omitting one or two words and replacing them with lines.

3. Print the missing words at the top, bottom, or on the opposite page for your child to copy. As her reading skills improve, make new books with longer text on each page.

☆ **Activity:**

1. Ask your child to read the story and write in the missing words. She
   can do the project all at once or over several days, according to her level
   of interest.

2. When the book is completed, invite her decorate the cover creatively.

3. Read the book together and add it to her library.

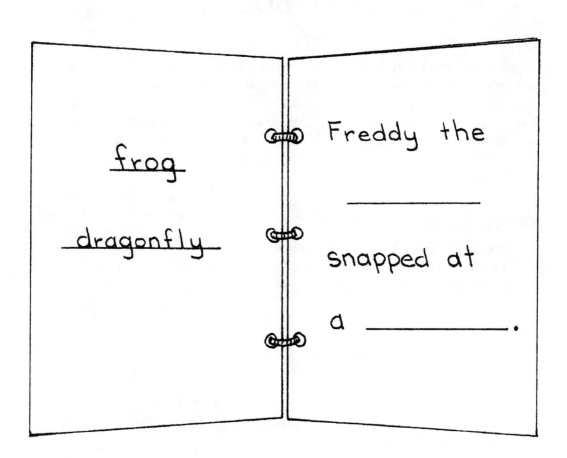

ꙮ 43 ꙮ

PARTNERS:

STORY BOOKS 1

As your child's vocabulary expands, make him storybooks with the new partner words learned in Lessons 39 and 40. The books are simple to create: just glue pictures that suggest a story onto paper, then add a few descriptive sentences. Although the sample sentences in this activity contain words that are beyond what is typically classified as beginning reading level, if your child has worked through the preceding lessons— particularly Lesson 40 (Partners: Long Vowel, Build a Word)—he should have no difficulty.

☞ **What You Need:**

Paper or cardstock; Partner Pictures (page 36) or other pictures or stickers, Short Vowel Words (page 93), Long Vowel Partner Words (page 156), scissors, glue, colored markers, hole punch, yarn

✂ **To Prepare:**

1. Cut paper or cardstock into six to ten pages. Punch holes in the sides and bind with yarn.

2. Choose Partner Pictures (or other pictures or stickers) and glue them onto the left-hand pages. Either arrange them to suggest a simple story or make each page an individual subject.

3. Use colored markers to write—on the right-hand pages—descriptive sentences to accompany the pictures. Refer to Short-Vowel Words and Long-Vowel Partner Words for ideas.

4. Write a title on the cover.

Examples:

- Picture: rock
  Sentences: Justin has a gray rock in his pocket. Can he toss the rock across the stream?

- Picture: bike
  Sentence: Mike rides his bike to visit five pals.

- Picture: bee
  Sentence: Seela sees three bees on the green tree.

- Picture: crayon
  Sentence: Ray plays with clay and crayons.

- Picture: robe
  Sentences: Meg got a gift. It is a robe with red roses on it.

- Picture: flute
  Sentence: The man played a lute, and the woman played the flute.

- Picture: bar of soap
  Sentence: Wash with soap, and then get a snack of toast.

- Picture: mailbox
  Sentences: Paint a picture on the card. Put it in the mailbox.

- Picture: key
  Sentences: Hide a key under the rock. Put another key in your pocket.

- Picture: candy cane
  Sentences: Candy canes are sweet treats. I like to eat them.

- Picture: doll
  Sentences: Sally is happy. She has sixty pretty fairy dolls.

- Picture: eight ball (billiards)
  Sentences: Hit the ball with the cue stick. The eight ball is the last ball to go in a pocket. The eight ball is black.

- Picture: calendar
  Sentences: May is when I plant potatoes and pick peas. In June I pick roses.

- Picture: toy boat
  Sentences: Janet made this little sailboat. It floats well. She will sail it in her bathtub.

- Picture: doll
  Sentences: Bethany has a pretty doll. The doll's name is Ellen. Ellen has a pink dress and pink socks. Bethany likes to brush her doll's hair.

- Picture: bottles of craft paint
  Sentences: Danny has a box of paints. He might paint his kite green. He might dilute the paint and brush it on his paper boat.

- Picture: a cat
  Sentences: The cat said mew and lapped milk from the pewter bowl. The dog continued to chew on a bone from the meat stew.

- Picture: a lime
  Sentences: Grandma's lime pie won a blue ribbon at the fair. Dad's wheat and honey muffins got high praise. I liked the peach pie and cheese pizza best.

- Picture: a tree
  Sentences: Hoe a square by the tree and plant the melons. We can see them grow from the window.

- Picture: a coat
  Sentences: Haylee wore the yellow coat when she went to feed the animals. She fed the foal and goat wheat, oats, and barley. She tossed grain to the chickens. The pigs got a bucket of scraps and sweet beets.

☆ Activity:

Have your child read you his books often and share them with friends.

❧ 44 ❧

PARTNERS:

STORY BOOKS 2

To make reading enticing and relevant, create short stories on subjects that appeal to your child. This project increases the word-to-picture ratio by having several pages of text to accompany one image. Surprise her with one of these handmade books, or have her choose a favorite picture and help you write the story.

☞ What You Need:

Assorted pictures, paper, cardstock, scissors, ruler, glue, pen or colored markers, hole punch, yarn

✂ To Prepare:

1. Cut a cardstock cover and paper pages. Punch holes along one edge and bind with yarn.

2. Write a title on the cover. Glue a picture on the front or inside of the cover.

3. Compose a story that relates to the picture, then copy it onto the pages.

Example:

Here is a story I created for our children, using a picture of ducks cut from a poultry catalog. The book had 4½- by 6-inch tagboard covers, 4¼- by 5-inch paper pages, and was written with blue ink pen.

Cover Title: 4 Ducks

Page 1: Picture of four white ducks.

Page 2: Betty has 4 ducks. The ducks are white and plump. Betty feeds her ducks grain.

Page 3: The ducks like the sun. The sun makes them hot. If the sun is too hot, the ducks go to the pond.

Page 4: The ducks swim in the pond. They snack on little fish. They dip their bills in the water and nibble plants too.

Page 5: After the swim, the 4 ducks waddle back to the grass.

Page 6: The ducks see bugs in the grass. The bugs make a fine snack for the ducks.

Page 7: (inside back cover): Betty likes to pet her ducks. They are soft and warm. Betty has 4 happy ducks.

☆ **Activity:**
Read the books together and add them to your child's library.

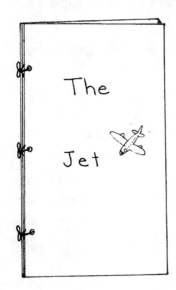

৵ 45 ৵

More Partners:

Book 1

With this activity, your child learns more letter partners and continues building his vocabulary by making a seven-page book of words.

☞ **What You Need:**

Colored copy or construction paper, Small Letter Cards (page 118), small writing paper (page 36), scissors, glue, black pen, colored and lead pencils, hole punch, yarn

✂ **To Prepare:**

1. For each page, cut writing paper to fit on a piece of colored paper, as shown on page 171, and glue together.

2. With a black pen, draw a vertical line from the top of the page to the bottom of the writing paper, as shown in the illustration.

3. Write the two partners *ar* and *or* with black ink at the top of the page. This is a Word Page. Repeat with the remaining six pairs of letter partners: *ie* and *ie, oo* and *oo, oi* and *oy, ou* and *ow, au* and *aw, ei* and *ei.* Use a different colored paper for each page.

4. On separate sheets of lined paper, write Word Lists for each set of letter partners, as shown below on the next page. Your child will copy these words onto the Word Pages.

Examples:
Here are partner Word Lists for the seven pages:

Page 1
ar: arm, artist, barn, charm, market, star, cart, dark, quart, tarnish

or: order, horn, corn, sort, form, forest, lord, story, stork, orchard

Page 2
ie: (sometimes says long-vowel *e):* field, grief, yield, thief, belief, chief, priest, fiend, shield, wield

ie: (sometimes says long-vowel *i):* pie, tie, lie, die, flies, dried, tries, spies, defies, fried

Page 3
oo: (sometimes sounds like *oo* in *moon):* moon, zoo, broom, balloon, raccoon, roof, tool, spool, noon, spoon

oo: (sometimes sounds like *u* in *put):* book, hook, look, took, cook, shook, brook, crook, foot, good

Page 4
oi: oil, soil, foil, moist, coil, boil, toil, oink, noise, hoist

oy: boy, Roy, toy, coy, joy, oyster, soy, enjoy, loyal, royal

Page 5
ou: out, pound, shout, mouth, snout, round, sour, flour, cloud, trout

ow: town, cow, clown, growl, owl, brown, how, crown, plow, howl

Page 6
au: automobile, author, haunt, Paul, jaunt, launch, August, dinosaur, sauce, vault

aw: dawn, lawn, awful, raw, hawk, paw, flaw, yawn, claw, strawberry

Page 7

Here's a classic saying that covers most *ie* and *ei* situations: *i* before *e*, except after *c*, or when sounded like *a* as in *neighbor* or *weigh*.

ei: neighbor, weigh, weight, veil

ei: ceiling, conceit, perceive, receive, deceive

☆ **Activity:**

1. Ask your child to build the two letter partners with the Small Letter Cards. For Page 1, this would be *ar* and *or*.

2. Give him a prepared Word Page and the matching Word List. Say the sounds of the letter partners and have him read the Word List. Discuss the meaning of any words he is not familiar with and look them up in a dictionary together.

3. Ask him to choose a colored pencil. Copying from the Word List, have him write the letter partners on the top set of lines and the words on the lines beneath, using colored pencil for the partners and lead pencil for the other letters. Encourage him to say each word as he prints it.

4. When all seven pages are completed, give the book a construction paper cover, punch holes down the sides, and bind with yarn. Write "More Partners: Book 1" on the cover. Suggest he read you the words, from time to time, for review.

ar	or
ar	or
arm	order
barn	horn
cart	corn
star	sort
charm	form
quart	lord
artist	story
partner	stork
market	border
tarnish	forest

MORE PARTNERS:

BOOKS 2, 3, 4, & 5

This important activity introduces more letter partners to help your child read and write a new collection of words. Have her work on the books in order—one page at a time. A sticker chart offers a fun way for her to track her progress.

☞ **What You Need:**

Colored paper, Small Letter Cards (page 118), small writing paper (page 36), scissors, glue, black pen, colored and lead pencils, stickers, hole punch, yarn

✄ **To Prepare: Word Pages**

1. For each page, cut a sheet of colored paper in half, lengthwise. Cut writing paper to fit on the piece of colored paper, as shown on page 174, and glue together. This is a Word Page.

2. Make a set of Word Pages for each book (see Examples on following pages), as your child is ready for them. Write one letter partner with black ink at the top of each Word Page.

3. Cut a construction paper cover and write the name of the book on it, for example, "Partners Book 2."

4. To help your child record her progress, make a simple sticker chart on the inside front cover or each booklet. Do this by writing a vertical row of letter partners in the order they appear in the book. Leave ample space between each letter partner, so there is room for a sticker next to it.

✂ To Prepare: Word Lists

On separate sheets of lined paper, write Word Lists for each set of letter partners, as shown below and on the following pages. Your child will copy these onto the Word Pages.

☆ Activity:

1. Begin with Page 1 of Partners Book 2: Five Pals, see below. Ask your child to build the first letter partner, *er,* with the Small Letter Cards.

2. Give her a Word Page and the Word List for *er.* Say the sounds of the partners and have her read the list. Discuss the meaning of any word she is not familiar with and look it up in a dictionary together. Say each word in a sentence.

3. Have her write the partners with colored pencil on the top set of lines on the Word Page. Next have her write the partner words on the lines beneath, using colored pencil for the letter partners and lead pencil for the other letters. Encourage her to say each word as she copies it.

4. As each page is finished, have her place a sticker on the Sticker Chart drawn on the inside front cover. When all the pages of Partners Book 2 are completed, punch two holes at the top and bind with yarn.

5. Follow the steps above to make Partner Book 3, 4, and 5. Encourage your child to do one page daily for reading, writing, and vocabulary practice. Occasionally ask her to read you previously finished books.

Examples: Partners Book 2: Five Pals

I call this book "Five Pals" because each set of letter partners has the *er* sound. Here are the Word Lists for Partners Book 2:

Page 1
er: her, term, summer, faster, fern, German, person, otter, under, sister

Page 2
ir: first, chirp, shirt, swirl, twirl, squirrel, firm, girl, stir, thirty

Page 3
ur: nurse, purse, burst, burn, turn, fur, hurry, scurry, lemur, curtain

Page 4

wor: work, word, world, worry, worst, worm

Page 5

ear: early, earn, earnest, pearl, learn, earth, Earl, yearn

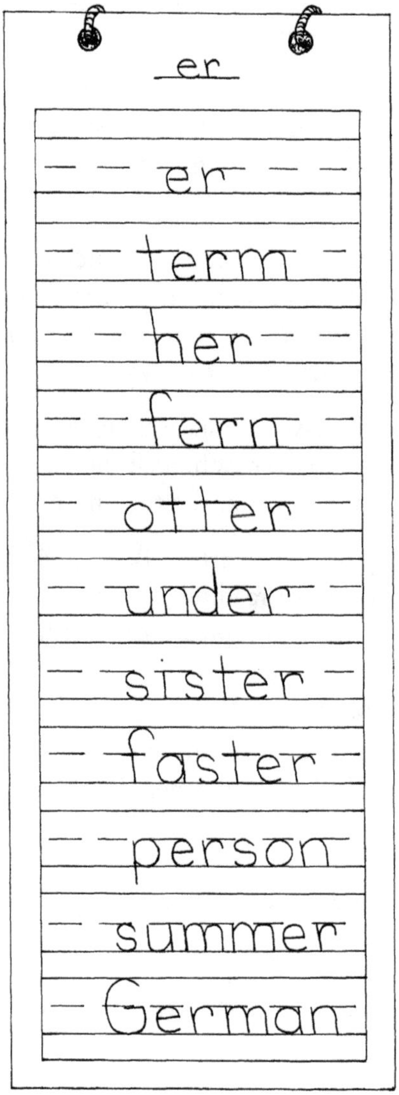

_er_

er
term
her
fern
otter
under
sister
faster
person
summer
German

Examples: Partners Book 3

Here are the Word Lists for Partners Book 3:

Page 1

kn (says *n*): knife, knight, knot, knit, knapsack, knee, kneel, knob, knock, know

Page 2

gn (says *n*): gnat, gnome, gnash, gnaw, gnu, reign, foreign

Page 3

wr (says *r*): write, wren, wrap, wreath, wreck, wrench, wring, wrist, wrong, wrote

Page 4

ph (says *f*): phone, pheasant, phonics, phony, photo, physical, Ralph, phosphorus

Page 5

gh (says *g*): ghost, gherkin, ghoul, Ghana, ghastly

Page 6

le (says *l*): apple, simple, handle, candle, puddle, fumble, warble, bottle, tentacle

Page 7

ng: song, long, hang, rang, sting, ring, swing, hung, spring, strung

Page 8

ck: luck, duck, packet, sack, pocket, bucket, wreck, locket, lick, sock

Page 9

ch (sometimes says *k*): chord, chorus, character, chrome, chrysalis, Chris, school, chrysanthemum, chromium, chemist

Page 10

ch: (sometimes says *sh*): chute, Chicago, charade, Cheyenne, chevron, chauffeur, chivalry, charlatan, chef, chartreuse

Examples: Partners Book 4

Here are Word Lists for Partners Book 4:

Page 1
all: fall, call, stall, small, squall, fall, hall, ball, tall, wallet

Page 2
ing: sing, string, swing, king, bring, wishing, digging, barking, wing, thing

Page 3
tch (says *ch)*: ditch, itch, match, latch, patch, stretch, fetch, catch, witch, switch

Page 4
dge (says *j)*: badge, badger, knowledge, hedge, fledge, bridge, ridge, Madge, edge, fudge

Page 5
y (sometimes says long-vowel *e):* Peggy, Freddy, many, sunny, valley, Billy, lily, chilly, chubby, hurry

Page 6
y (sometimes says long-vowel *i):* by, try, shy, ply, lyre, pylon, nylon, typist, dynamite, tyrannosaur

Page 7
y (sometimes says short-vowel *i):* symbol, symphony, syrup, lynx, gypsy, typical, myth, nymph, gymnasium, mystery

Page 8
ed (sometimes says *ed):* traded, planted, sanded, weeded, painted, braided, hunted, counted

Page 9
ed (sometimes says *d):* sunned, dried, filled, brushed, colored, burned, feathered, canned, bathed

Page 10

ed (sometimes says *t*)*:* pecked, plucked, wrecked, washed, flashed, polished, locked, licked

Examples: Partners Book 5

On Pages 4–9, below, point out that *c* and *g* often say their "soft" sounds, *s* and *j,* when followed by the letters *e, i,* or *y*. Here are Word Lists for Partners Book 5:

Page 1

ci (sometimes says *sh)*: special, commercial, financial, facial, racial, glacial, spacious, ancient

Page 2

ti (sometimes says *sh)*: nation, station, vacation, position, addition, education, subtraction, motion, solution, mention

Page 3

si (sometimes says *sh* or *zh)*: mission, division, session, pension, vision

Page 4

ce: center, celebrate, century, cement, cell, cent

Page 5

ci: circle, circus, cider, city, citrus, cinnamon, cinder

Page 6

cy (notice that the *y* can say either the long- or short-*i* sound): cycle, encyclopedia, cypress, cygnet, cylinder, bicycle, tricycle

Page 7

ge: gem, gel, gelatin, genuine, gesture, gentle, refrigerator, pigeon

Page 8

gi (notice that the *i* can say either its long or short sound): giant, gigantic, ginger, giraffe, gibberish, gingerbread

Page 9

gy (notice that the y can say either the long- or short-*i* sound):
gyroscope, gym, gymnasium, gypsum, gypsy

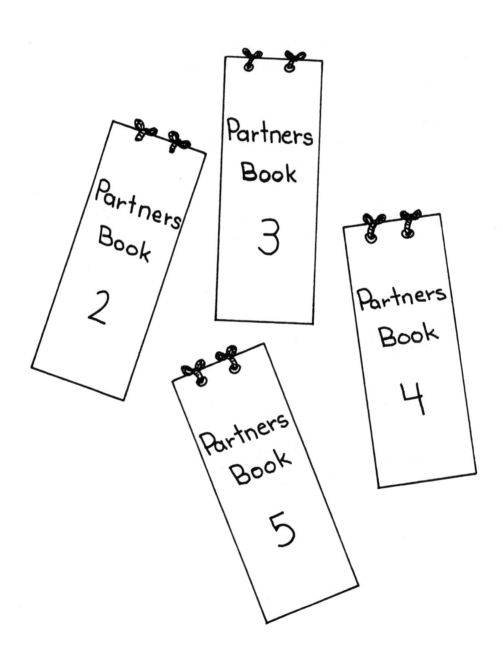

❧ 47 ❧

MORE PARTNERS:

"OUGH" CHART

Make a wall chart to illustrate the peculiar qualities of the four-letter partners, ough. *Have your child read the chart often to familiarize himself with the six different sounds of* ough, *the "master of disguise."*

☞ **What You Need:**

Construction paper or cardstock, small writing paper (page 36), pen, colored markers, tape, scissors, basket or envelope

✄ **To Prepare:**

1. Draw the "ough Chart" on a piece of construction paper or cardstock, adding lines and labels, as shown on page 181.

2. Cut fifteen one-word-sized slips of paper or cardstock and place them in a basket or envelope. These will become Word Cards.

☆ **Activity 1:**

1. Set the chart on a table or on the floor. Bring out the Word Cards.

2. Write the letters *ough* on a piece of lined writing paper. Explain that these letter partners make six different sounds: *o* as in *note*, *oo* as in *moon*, *uf* as in *cuff*, *off* as in *cough*, *o* as in *hot*, *ow* as in *cow*. Make a fun challenge of saying the six sounds of *ough* in a series. Repeat several times.

Sounds of *ough:*
o: long-vowel *o,* as in *note.*
oo: as in *moon.*
uf: as in *cuff.*
off: as in *cough.*
o: short-vowel *o,* as in *hot.*
ow: as in *cow.*

3. Give your child the lined paper. Explain that you are going to say words with the first *ough* sound, *o* (as in *note*). Pronounce the first word, *though*. Ask your child to listen carefully to the sounds and write what he hears, using the *ough* letter partners.

4. Say the next word, *dough,* and again have him listen and write it. Repeat with the word *although*.

5. Have him read the three words he has written. Ask him to print them onto three Word Cards and place them in the first column of the *ough* Chart.

6. Repeat steps 2–4 for the remaining five sounds of *ough*. Do this project all at once or over several days, depending on his interest. When the day's session is finished, ask him to remove the Word Cards from the chart and replace them in the basket or envelope. Continue to say the six sounds of *ough* often.

☆ **Activity 2:**

1. When all the Word Cards have been made and all the sounds introduced, set the *ough* Chart on a table and place the Word Cards at random below it. Invite your child to choose a card, read it, and place it in the correct column on the chart. Do this once or several times over a few days. Chant the six sounds of *ough* together.

2. When you feel that he is comfortable with the *ough* words, have him tape the Word Cards onto the chart in their proper columns and hang it on a wall or bulletin board. Encourage him to read the chart out loud.

Examples:

Here are word lists for the *ough* chart:

- *ough* that says long-vowel *o,* as in note: though, dough, although

- *ough* that says *oo,* as in moon: through

- *ough* that says *uf,* as in cuff: rough, tough, enough

- *ough* that says *off:* cough, slough

- *ough* that says short-vowel *o,* as in hot: ought, fought, sought, thought, bought

- *ough* that says *ow,* as in cow: bough, plough
  (Note: plough is a British variation of *plow)*

The six sounds of "ough"					
ō	oo	uf	off	ŏ	ow
though		rough		ought	bough
		tough		bought	
		enough			

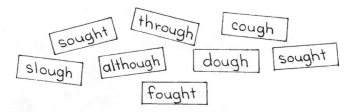

❦ 48 ❧

Nature Book

Now that your child is familiar with short vowel and partner words, she needs to practice using them. Nature Book provides whimsical reading material that incorporates a variety of new words. Make the books yourself and offer them as a surprise, or invite her to help create them.

☞ **What You Need:**

Paper or cardstock, pictures of plants and animals, scissors, glue, colored markers, hole punch, yarn

✂ **To Prepare:**

1. Cut paper or cardstock into six to ten rectangular pages. Punch holes in the sides and bind with yarn.

2. Collect pictures or stickers of plants or animals. Affix the pictures onto the left pages.

3. Invent a short rhyme or paragraph to describe each image. Use colored markers to write the sentences on the right pages.

4. Print a title on the cover.

☆ **Activity:**

Give your child the Nature Book. Invite her to read it to you and to her friends.

Examples:

- Picture of a bee:

    The smell of pollen calls the bee.
    It makes honey for you and me.

- Picture of a panther:

    Be watchful and careful
    A panther is waiting,
    It prowls in the bushes
    And plays in the sun.

    The Florida panther may
    Look like a kitty,
    But if you should see one
    Be ready to run!

- Picture of a spotted owl:

    Spotted owl
    Your eyes are big
    I spy you sitting
    On a twig.

    In the forest
    Where you fly,
    Drop me a feather
    As you sail by.

- Picture of a zebra:

    Zebra, zebra
    In the park,
    Your stripes are
    Very bright.

    I'd like to brush
    Your pretty coat,
    But you might
    Kick or bite.

- Picture of a polar bear:

  Come north with me
  To the arctic cold,
  Where we can see
  The polar bear bold!

- Picture of a starfish:

  In a little tidepool
  By the vast sea,
  Lives a little starfish
  Happy and free!

- Picture of large spoonbill birds:

  These are pink spoonbills
  Their feathers are bright,
  In Florida people can
  See them in flight.

- Picture of a whale:

  The whale lives deep in the ocean,
  The whale lives deep in the sea,
  The whale dives deep in the water,
  Oh whale come play with me.

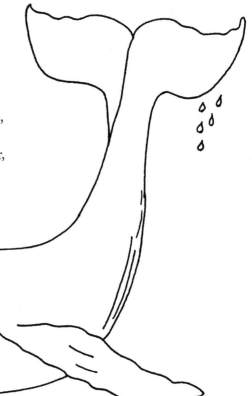

NUMBER WORD CHART

This fun chart helps your child learn the number words. Build it one word per day or all in one session, depending on his level of interest.

☞ What You Need:

Colored copy or construction paper, small writing paper (page 36), colored pencils, colored markers, scissors, tape, twenty assorted stickers

✄ To Prepare:

1. Draw a line at the top of a sheet of colored paper. Write "Number Word Chart" on the line.

2. Draw six dots, evenly spaced, down the left side of the page, as shown on the illustration.

3. On a second sheet of paper, draw eight evenly-spaced dots down the left side.

4. On a third sheet of paper, again draw eight evenly-spaced dots down the left side. Cut off any excess from the bottom, leaving a comfortable space under the last dot.

5. Tape the three sheets to a wall or bulletin board, one above the other.

☆ Activity:

1. With your child watching, write the word *one* on a piece of lined writing paper.

2. Instruct him to copy it two times for practice, then write it "his very best" with colored pencil or marker.

3. Have him cut out the number word and tape it onto the chart to the right of the topmost dot. Invite him to get a sticker and place it on the dot.

4. Repeat steps 1–3 for the numbers 2 through 20. Have him count down the stickers each time he applies one.

☙ 50 ☙

CALENDAR FELT BOARD

Teach your child how to write the days of the week and the months of the year with this project, then use the calendar to track the flow of time. Take a few minutes each morning to give your child a smile and a hug, change the date on the Calendar Felt Board, and discuss the day's activities.

☞ What You Need:

Cardboard or posterboard, small writing paper (page 36), cardstock, white or colored paper, self-adhesive felt (or use regular felt and glue), glue, ruler, scissors, colored markers, soft-lead colored pencils, calendar, basket or box

✂ To Prepare:

1. Cut cardboard or posterboard into a 10- by 18-inch rectangle.

2. Cut a 4½- by 18-inch piece of self-adhesive felt. Peel off the backing and press it onto the top part of the board.

3. Prepare white or colored paper as follows to make three pockets, as shown on the next page:

   • For pockets 1 and 2, cut two 4¼- by 5½-inch pieces of paper.

   • For pocket 3, cut one 2¾- by 4¼-inch rectangle of paper.

4. Fold the three pockets ½-inch along two sides and the bottom. With a colored marker, write "Days of the week" on pocket 1; "Months of the year" on pocket 2; and "Year" on pocket 3.

5. Spread glue along the folded flaps and press onto the board, as shown. Make sure you only affix the side and bottom edges of the pockets.

6. Cut cardstock as follows to make movable labels:

- Nineteen 1- by 4½-inch labels for the days of the week and months of the year.

- Thirty-one 1- by 1¾-inch labels for the numerical dates.

- Two or three 1- by 3-inch labels for the years.

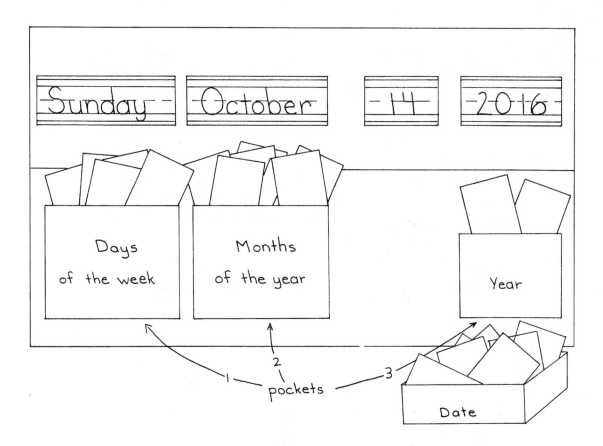

☆ **Activity:**

1. Look at a calendar with your child. Read the names of the days of the week and then count them. Flip through the pages of the calendar and read the names of the months and notice how many days each month has. Explain that today she will make a calendar of her own, one that she can update daily.

2. Ask her to write, with bright colored pencils or markers, the days of the week onto lined writing paper. Refer her to the calendar to check her spelling. If she makes mistakes, have her copy the words correctly.

3. Invite her to cut out the days-of-the-week words and glue them onto the seven prepared 1- by 4½-inch labels. Cut seven strips of felt to fit on the back of the labels and invite her to stick them on. Place the finished labels in pocket 1.

4. Now, or on a later day, have her:

    a. Write the names of the months and glue them on the remaining 1- by 4½-inch labels. Back the labels with felt and place them in pocket 2.

    b. Write the numbers 1–31 on the 1- by 1¾-inch labels. Back the labels with felt and place them in a basket or box.

    c. Write the current and coming years on the 1- by 1¾-inch labels. Back the labels with felt and place them in pocket 3.

4. Attach the Calendar Felt Board to a wall or keep it accessible on a shelf. Place the basket or box of numbers nearby. Consult a calendar, then invite her to place the labels to form the correct date on the Calendar Felt Board. Remind her to change the date daily.

↬ 51 ↬

Helping Words 3:
Mystery Words

This activity will expand your child's vocabulary and familiarize him with words that present spelling challenges. It also gives him the opportunity to invent and write sentences himself. The decorated Mystery Words box and folded papers add an element of fun!

☞ **What You Need:**

Box, construction paper, glue, colored markers, colored paper, small writing paper (page 36), scissors, lead or colored pencils.

✄ **To Prepare:**

1. Decorate the box with construction paper and colored markers. Write *Mystery Words* on the side.

2. Cut up the colored paper (eight pieces per sheet works well) and write sets of words on them. See examples on the next page.

3. Fold the papers into quarters and place them into the box.

Examples:

Mystery Words 1

- come, some fruit, suit
- climb, limb, comb
- none, done, some, son
- laugh, aisle, doubt
- should, would, could
- height, ocean, movie
- answer, sword, toward
- hair, their, give
- how, when, why, wavy
- machine, unique, you
- piano, violin, cello, music
- gravy, shady, ladle
- cobra, hold, roll
- thyme, juice, soup

Mystery Words 2

- walk, talk, calm, palm
- sugar, sure, measure, usual
- who, shoe, jewelry
- woman, women, people
- build, unit, huge
- human, pupil, library
- colonel, bugle, union
- humor, menu, fury
- great, steak, break
- baby, lady, table, love
- find, kind, mind
- gold, sold, cold, soda
- head, deaf, tongue
- straight, guess, friend

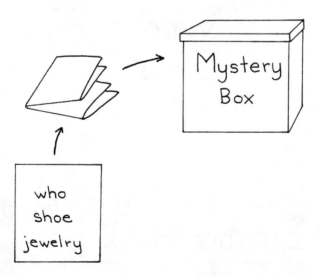

☆ **Activity:**

1. Show your child the Mystery Words Box. Explain that it holds sets of useful words that he should become familiar with. We call them *mystery* words because they don't necessary follow the rules he has learned.

2. Invite him to take a folded paper from the Mystery Words Box and read the words aloud. If one is unfamiliar, show him how to consult a dictionary to find the definition.

3. Ask him to print each word two times onto a fresh sheet of writing paper, then write a sentence using one or more of the new words. Suggest he write it in secret. When finished, he can surprise you by reading it aloud. Congratulate him on a job well done!

   Note: Silently make note of any misspelled words in the sentence. Don't mention them now. By doing so, you could dampen your child's sense of accomplishment or make him hesitant to write, for fear of "doing it wrong." Simply present the words in a fresh lesson on another day, see Spelling Cards, page 239.

4. Have him do one Mystery Words set per day. When he completes fourteen pages, add a construction paper cover and staple down the side to form a book. Title it "Mystery Words 1." Do the same with the last fourteen pages and title it "Mystery Words 2."

who who
shoe shoe
jewelry jewelry

Who put my jewelry
in the shoe?

❧ 52 ❧

PARTNERS:

STORY BOOKS 3

Help your child's reading ability improve by offering homemade books that gradually increase in difficulty. Now that she is familiar with most of the phonetic sounds, you have freedom to craft stories without constraining yourself to certain words. If you feel it would be beneficial, of course, you can also emphasize certain phonetic letter patterns.

Make the stories informative, humorous, or mysterious. Invent tales about family, friends, and pets to spark her enthusiasm. Or focus on her life and interests. Including her in some of the adventures will make her curious to see what "she" is doing on each new page.

☞ **What You Need:**
Lined notebook paper, report covers or construction paper, pen, hole punch and yarn (optional)

✄ **To Prepare:**
1. Write short stories on sheets of lined notebook paper, one per page. Bind a collection of them in a report cover with fasteners or add a construction paper cover, punch holes, and bind with yarn.

2. Make several of these books and title them "Reading Book 1," "Reading Book 2," etc., or give them unique titles.

Examples:

Here are some story and thematic ideas to get you started:

- Use the short vowels sounds: *a, e, i, o, u.* (See Short Vowel Words, page 93.)

- Include lots of consonant blends, such as *th, ch, sh,* or *wh.*

- Focus on the long vowel sounds. (See Long Vowel Partner Words, page 156).

    a: cane, rain, play, sleigh

    e: feel, seat, key, happy

    i: pine, pie, night, dry

    o: home, toe, boat, row

    u: mule, blue, new

- Describe your child's daily activities, a special event, or an adventure.

- Use the names of family members and friends.

- Include family pets.

- Describe the adventures of a favorite cartoon character.

- Narrate an imaginary trip.

- Write from the point of view of an object in your house or of a favorite toy that comes to life.

- Explain the steps needed to do something, such as bake a cake, wash a car, grow a pumpkin, prepare for a piano or dance recital, take an airline trip, wash a dog, build a house, or paint a picture.

- Describe the life of a famous person or share an anecdote from a family member or friend.

- Follow the activities of a family member or friend for one day.

- Prepare your child for an upcoming event.

- Describe a picture that you glue on the page with the story.

☆ **Activity:**

Read the books together and add them to your child's library.

৵ 53 ৵

PARTNERS:

WRITING SENTENCES

This activity reinforces reading, writing, and thinking skills as your child uses Partner Words in sentences. It also introduces the comma. (For more information about comma usage, see Punctuation Guide, page 324.)

☞ **What You Need:**

Small writing paper (page 36), Partner Pictures (page 36), Small Letter Cards (page 118), three-minute timer, construction paper, scissors, hole punch, yarn

✂ **To Prepare:**

1. Cut the writing paper into strips with four sets of writing lines.

2. Cut construction paper rectangles slightly larger than the writing paper.

3. Print and cut out some partner pictures that suggest sentences.

☆ **Activity:**

1. With your child, write a sentence that requires a comma. Explain that commas mean that the reader should pause. Read each sentence aloud with your child, emphasizing the pause after the comma.

Examples:

- "Tom, put the cat outside," said Dad.

- Mom said, "Please set the table for dinner."

- The yarn was green, blue, red, and yellow.

- That book was good, but I thought it was too short.

Note: Commas are used to separate items in a list; before some conjunctions, such as and and but; and to set off names and direct quotes. While your child doesn't need to know all the details at this point, he should become familiar with its use in basic writing. This is also a good time to show him how to place quotation marks around direct quotes.

2. Bring the Small Letter Cards and Partner Pictures to a table. Invite your child to choose a Partner Picture, say its name, and then try to spell it verbally. Assist him if he needs help. Tell him a sentence that you invent based on the picture, then ask him build it with the Small Letter Cards. Set the three-minute timer and leave.

Examples:
Here are two sample sentences for each picture. The first is easier, the second is more difficult. You would say only one sentence, not both.

- Picture: slide
  Sentences: The slide in the park is fast.
  > or
  The park has six swings, three slides, and a pool.

- Picture: candy
  Sentences: Jenny got a gift of candy.
  > or
  I bought Josh a chocolate candy bar.

- Picture: goat
  Sentences: The goat ate my hat.
  > or
  Nanny goats are nice, but Billy goats are gruff.

- Picture: robe
  Sentences: Nan has a soft pink robe.

  or

  Jessica's robe is pink, yellow, and white.

- Picture: chewing
  Sentences: Rick chews green gum.

  or

  "Chew with your mouth closed," Sam.

3. At the end of three minutes, or sooner if he calls you, look at the sentence he formed. Help him with any difficult words, then have him write the sentence on the lined paper.

4. Have him glue the paper onto a construction paper rectangle. Set it aside to dry. Invite him to choose another picture and repeat steps 2–4.

5. Encourage him do one to three pages daily in short sessions until ten pages are completed. Invite him to decorate a construction paper cover, then punch holes down the side and bind with yarn.

6. Read the book together and add it to his library. Suggest he read the book to friends.

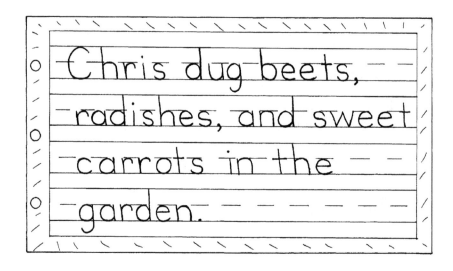

❧ 54 ❧

PARTNERS:

DEFINITION BOOKS

Here's a great way to introduce new words while providing additional reading practice.

☞ **What You Need:**

Paper or cardstock, pictures or stickers, scissors, glue, colored markers, hole punch, yarn

✄ **To Prepare:**

1. Cut paper or cardstock into pages, varying their size and color in different books for variety. Punch holes in the sides and bind with yarn.

2. Collect pictures or stickers (or draw images yourself). Focus on a theme, such as dinosaurs, mushrooms, airplanes, berries, horses, African animals, root vegetables, trees, cars, whales, insects, planets, etc.

3. Glue the illustrations onto the left-hand pages.

4. Write a short definition (or a few sentences that tell a bit of story and give some new information) on the right-hand pages.

Variation:

For very early readers, make one-page books with folded pieces of cardstock.

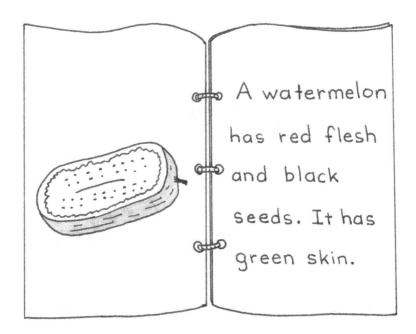

Examples:

- Picture: kelp
  Sentences: This is kelp. It lives in the sea. We can eat it.

- Picture: polar bear playing with cubs
  Sentences: The bears have thick fur coats to keep them warm. Cubs play near mom.

- Picture: heron
  Sentences: A heron has a long neck. Herons feed in swamps.

- Picture: fish
  Sentences: A fish has fins to help it swim. Can you swim as fast as a fish?

- Picture: a tree
  Sentences: This green tree lives in a forest. Birds build nests in it.

- Picture: crab
  Sentences: This is a crab. It lives on a sandy beach. It eats kelp and small fish. It has eight legs and two big claws.

- Picture: a bird
  Sentences: A bird has a beak, wings, and a tail. It has feathers and can fly. It lays eggs. It is not a mammal.

☆ **Activity:**

Invite your child to read the Definition Books to you and add them to her library. Encourage her to read them to her friends and family.

MORE ACTION STICKERS

Use Action Stickers as rewards for completing tasks. They give your child a quick break from seated work and another reason to read.

☞ **What You Need:**

Large blank stickers, pen, container (such as a pretty bowl, basket, or box)

✂ **To Prepare:**

1. Write short phrases with directions on the stickers. Here are some Action Sticker ideas:

- Count to twenty.

- Find Texas on a map.

- Find Paris on a map.

- Find Argentina on a flat map and on a globe.

- Pick up a bit of trash.

- Give Dad a hug.

- Give Mom a kiss.

- Touch your toes.

- Kick a ball.

- Brush the dog.

- Do a forward roll.

- Jump ten times.

- Swing your arms.

- Name five colors.

- Go hop!

2. Place the Action Stickers in a pretty bowl, basket, or box.

☆ **Activity:**
Action Stickers are great little rewards for finishing worksheets or booklets. When your child completes an assignment, say, "That's great! Go get an Action Sticker." He chooses one, reads it, does the indicated action, and then sticks it on his completed page or project.

PART 4

BUILDING VOCABULARY

At this level, your child knows the short and long sounds of the vowels and is familiar with letter partners. She is reading simple story books and writing sentences.

Part 4 builds on this foundation with fun activities that improve reading and writing skills while expanding vocabulary. After a step-by-step introduction to cursive writing, students learn how to compose paragraphs, and then put their new skills to work crafting stories.

Spelling Notebook (Lesson 68) offers a simple system for improving spelling. Homeschooling parents often fall back on traditional classroom techniques—such as spelling bees and tests—to teach this subject. While these methods may be useful for some children, they don't necessarily work well in a homeschool environment. We developed the Spelling Notebook as a tool for independent study and memorization. It uses reading, spelling aloud, and writing to engage multiple senses and train motor skills. The notebook also provides word lists that students can refer to for writing projects.

As your child works through these lessons, remember to visit the library often so she can choose intriguing books to read for pleasure.

❧ 56 ❧

HOW MANY WORDS?

As your child places descriptive words around a picture—such as a person, animal, vehicle, landmark, or food—she expands her vocabulary. Suggest she research the subject online or in a book. How many related words can she find?

☞ **What You Need:**

Construction paper, bulletin board (or poster board or large piece of construction paper), colored markers, scissors, dictionary

✂ **To Prepare:**

1. Attach a picture of an interesting item to a bulletin board.

2. Cut rectangles of brightly-colored construction paper. Make them large enough for your child to write words or short phrases on them.

☆ **Activity:**

1. Discuss the picture with your child, then ask her to say three words or phrases that describe it.

2. Have her write the words or phrases on the slips of construction paper and attach them next to the illustration. Remind her to use a dictionary to check the spelling of difficult words.

3. If she is happily engaged with the project, suggest she continue to find, write, and attach words around the picture. If interest is moderate or low, conclude the work. On another day, cheerfully challenge her to find three new words or phrases to add to the display.

❧ 57 ❧

Alphabet Word Games

Fun for two or more players, these simple games help your child expand his vocabulary and improve his mental dexterity.

☞ **What You Need:**

Small Letter Cards (page 118), basket or bag, paper, pencil or pen, timer

☆ **Game 1:**

1. Place one each of the Small Letter Cards *a, b, c, d, f, g, h, k, l, m, n, p, r, s, t, v,* and *w* into a basket or bag. Give each player a piece of paper and pencil or pen.

2. Have the first player draw a letter card, for example, *b,* and show it to the others. Set the timer for 30 seconds, 1 minute, or 3 minutes.

3. Players take turns saying the names of words (or phrases) that begin with the chosen letter: *bread, basket, bacon, bear, barn, bullet, bark, beast, barley, burst, banana bread, beautiful, breakfast,* etc. The game proceeds quickly. If a person cannot think of a word within a few seconds, the next player may say a word. Each person puts a mark on his page for each new word he says. The round concludes when the timer rings.

4. To continue, repeat steps 2 and 3. The game is over after a predetermined time or when participants decide to stop. At that point, each player counts up his marks, allotting one point per mark. The person with the highest number wins.

Variation:

Have players silently write as many words as they can within the given time. Each word that more than one person wrote is given one point. Words that are unique to a player's list are awarded two points.

☆ **Game 2:**

Same as Game 1, but have the first player choose a *category* (food, cars, animals, countries, sports, flowers, furniture, etc.) in addition to the letter. Once the game has ended, if your child has a special interest in a certain topic, help him search online or in books to learn new words related to it.

Examples:

- Letter *b:*
  Category, *food:* bananas, bacon, bread, beets, borscht, bread pudding, banana cake, banana ice cream, banana pancakes, beef, bagels, basil, barley, beans, blackberries, blueberries, broccoli, butter, brownies, butterscotch pudding, buttermilk pancakes, burritos

- Letter *m:*
  Category, *insects:* mayflies, monarch butterflies, moths, mosquitoes, mantis (praying), mites, midges, milkweed bugs, mourning cloak butterfly, Mexican bean beetle

- Letter *p:*
  Category, *trees:* pine, ponderosa pine, poplar, plum, pecan, pear, peach, papaya, palm, persimmon

- Letter *h:*
  Category, *animals:* hare, horse, hippopotamus, hairy woodpecker, hen, halibut, horseshoe crab, horned lizard, horned owl, hamster, hermit crab

- Letter *c:*
  Category, *countries:* Canada, China, Chile, Congo, Cuba, Costa Rica, Croatia, Cuba, Columbia, Czech Republic

- Letter *t:*
  Category, *clothes:* top hat, top coat, trousers, T-shirt, trench coat, tie, turban, tutu, tap shoes, toga, tiara, toe shoes, tights, tuxedo, tank top, tunic, turtleneck top, tennis shoes, train (a long skirt)

- Letter *a:*
  Category, *girls' names:* Anne, Amy, Angela, Amelia, Annie, Allison, Amaryllis, Amber, Alaina, Alice, Aster, April, Adrianne, Angelica, Ashley, Annette, Alexia, Alexandra, Abigail, Arlene, Arliss, Audrey, Autumn, Angel, Athena, Agnes, Agatha, Arielle, Amanda

☆ **Game 3:**

Put a complete alphabet set of Small Letter Cards into the basket or bag. Follow the directions for Game 1, with this change: Let the first player choose the letter and a *subject* that begins with that letter. Players then say or write words beginning with *any* letter connected to the given subject.

Examples:

- Letter, *e:*
  Subject, *Egypt:* pyramids, Nile River, pharaohs, sun, desert, sand, hot, fields, delta, King Tut, palm trees, dates, oases, camels, robes, King's Chamber, mummies, grain, hieroglyphics, museum

- Letter *d:*
  Subject, *dogs:* bark, fur, black, white, wet tongue, wag, tail, friendly, wiggly, brush, food, water, hunt, fetch, fleas, playful, sit, stay, leash, walk, run, jump, collar, vet, poodle, Labrador, beagle, terrier, collie, Great Dane, Chihuahua, cocker spaniel, husky, dalmatian

- Letter *v:*
  Subject *violin:* music, strings, wood, bow, handcrafted, polished, case, orchestra, players, Vivaldi, Beethoven, fiddle, country music, dancing, waltzes, music lessons, performance, practice

- Letter *r:*
  Subject *rocks:* hard, brown, red, blue, green, polished, gems, rings, buildings, monuments, necklaces, gravel, volcanoes, mountains, rock collection, minerals, granite, shale, limestone, obsidian, ruby, amethyst, emerald, coal, chalk, rock salt, diamond, sapphire

- Letter *o:*
  Subject *ocean:* water, seaweed, salt, big, vast, ships, boats, sailboats, submarines, fish, starfish, whales, seals, sea lions, seagulls, crabs, clams, shrimp, tuna, sea horses, shore, sand, sand dollars, tide pools, mermaids, sunken treasure, islands, adventure

❧ 58 ❧

LETTER ADD-UP GAME

This quick, easy game reviews spelling words while teaching thinking skills. It can brighten the mood and be a nice diversion from a longer project. The game also makes a fine travel activity.

☞ **What You Need:**

Paper, pencils or pens

☆ **Activity:**

This game is for two players. Decide on a time limit or on a number of rounds before the score is counted. Or just play for fun.

1. Give each player a piece of paper and pencil or pen. Set an additional sheet, called the Game Paper, between the participants. Player 1 thinks of a word and writes it on her paper, which she keeps hidden. She then writes the first *letter* of her word onto the Game Paper.

2. Player 2 thinks of a word that begins with the letter written on the Game Paper. She writes the word on her hidden paper, then adds the second letter of her word to the Game Paper.

3. The game progresses as Player 1 adds the third letter to the word, Player 2 adds the fourth letter, and so on, until a player can no longer think of a way to continue. With every turn, the player writes the word she is thinking of on her hidden paper.

4. When the round is finished, players show their hidden papers to share the words they were thinking of. The person who added the last letter takes the Game Paper.

5. When all rounds are concluded, the one who has collected the most
   Game Papers wins.

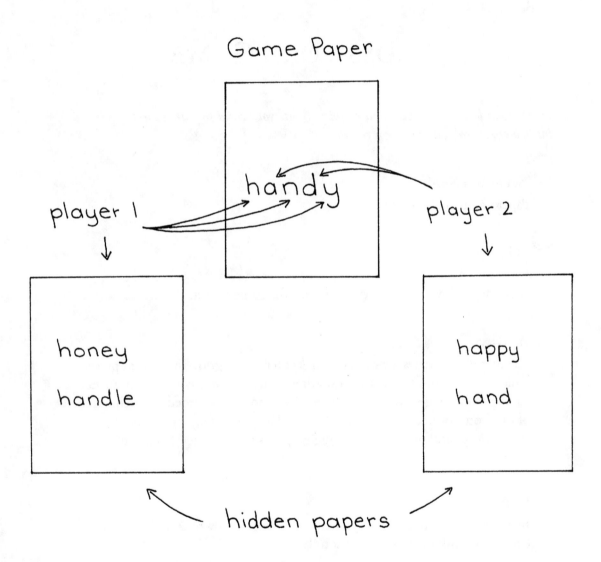

❧ 59 ❧

CROSSWORD GAME

Here's a fun language enrichment activity! Invite your child to grab a sheet of paper and build a crossword with you or a friend.

☞ **What You Need:**

Paper and pencils or pens

✄ **To Prepare:**

Draw a grid of squares on a sheet of paper, as shown. Make it smaller or larger depending on how long you want the game to last.

☆ **Activity:**

The first player writes a word near the center of the grid. The second player builds a word onto the first one, sharing a letter. Players continue, in turn, adding to existing words on the board. One point is awarded for each letter of the word formed, including the letter that was already on the paper. If two words are formed at right angles, points are awarded for the letters of both.

Variation:

Invite your child to create a crossword puzzle of his own, complete with clues and blank squares. See Lesson 89.

		c	a	b	b	a	g	e	
f	l	a	t		e		o		
		t			a			p	
	t		h	a	n	d		l	
	r	o	e			e	y	e	s
	u		a			n		a	t
	c	a	r	p	e	t		s	o
	k		t	o			h	e	n
				t	i	n			e

✌ 60 ✌

PHOTO BOOKS

Here is a delightful way to preserve childhood memories. Your child will love reading booklets that record events she has experienced and that tell stories about her friends and family.

☞ **What You Need:**

Cardstock, scissors, glue, colored markers, hole punch, yarn. Pictures taken during an outing or family gathering, holiday celebration, birthday party, or other event

✄ **To Prepare:**

Either make the book as a surprise or invite your child to choose the pictures and write the sentences. Follow these steps to make books on different subjects.

1. Cut cardstock into pages. Punch holes in the sides and bind with yarn.

2. Arrange photos for the book. Glue them onto the left-hand pages.

3. On facing pages, write a sentence or paragraph to accompany each picture.

☆ **Activity:**

Encourage your child to read the books often and share them with her friends.

Example 1: Birthday Party

Here are sample pages from a Birthday Book. Help your child record her own once-in-a-lifetime events, so she can read about them again and again.

- Picture: a smiling birthday child
  Sentences: Brianna is seven years old today. She is having a party!

- Picture: Mom and birthday cake
  Sentences: Her mom made her a beautiful chocolate birthday cake. It had white frosting and a ballerina on top.

- Picture: friends and presents
  Sentences: Brianna's friends, Mary, Paul, Evan, Nicole, and Katrina, came to the party. They brought gifts, played games, and ate cake.

- Picture: guests playing Pin the Tail on the Donkey
  Sentences: Her dad organized the games. Evan stuck the donkey's tail on its nose!

- Picture: birthday child and guests
  Sentences: Everyone had a fun time. Katrina told funny stories about her new puppy. Paul taught Brianna how to fold a paper crane.

Weston has 5 candles on his birthday cake.

Example 2: Zoo Pictures

- Picture: gorilla
  Sentence: Gorillas eat lots of bananas.

- Picture: leopards
  Sentence: Leopards have spots on their fur.

- Picture: flamingo
  Sentence: Flamingos have pink feathers.

- Picture: elephant
  Sentence: The elephant can flap his big ears.

- Picture: guinea hens
  Sentence: The guinea hens peck for seeds.

Variation 1:

To make a Family Photo Book, include a picture of each relative and write a few sentences about them.

Variation 2:

Instead making of a book, invite your child to create a poster with the pictures, adding funny "cartoon-balloon" comments for each one.

❧ 61 ❧

ACCORDION MYSTERY SLIPS

Discovering clues to a mystery item makes reading irresistible. Create a basketful of these booklets for extra reading practice or hand them out singly as rewards for good work.

☞ **What You Need:**

White or colored paper, scissors, ruler, pen or colored markers

✂ **To Prepare:**

1. Cut strips of white or assorted colored paper into 2- by 11-inch lengths.

2. Fold each strip in half, and then in thirds. Press the folds. Open the strip and refold accordion fashion (back and forth) along the folds you already made. You should now have an accordion strip with six sections. (See illustration on the next page.)

3. Fold up the slip and write on the top "Who Am I?" or "What Am I." Flip the booklet over and write the answer on the back. Then print a clue on each interior section. Secure with a paper clip and place in a basket.

Examples:

- What am I? I am brown. I have a tail. I like to sniff the ground. I like to dig. I have a wet tongue. I bark when I am excited. I am a dog.

- Who am I? I help people. I ride a big truck. I wear a red hat. I climb tall ladders. I slide down poles. I carry big water hoses. I am a fireman.

- What am I? I am very tall. I live outdoors. I have a trunk. Birds nest in me. My roots hold me in the ground. My leaves catch sunlight. I am a tree.

- What am I? I hide in a closet. I plug in the wall. You push me around. I clean things. I make a loud roar. I eat dirt. I am a vacuum cleaner.

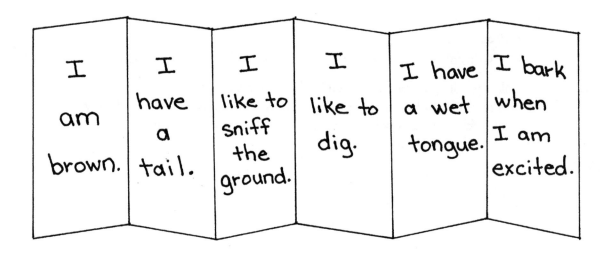

☆ **Activity:**

Ask your child to choose an Accordion Mystery Slip and read it. Have him try to guess what the mystery item is before he looks at the answer on the back. Encourage him to read the slips to friends and family.

RHYME BOOKS

Rhyming words bring a charming touch to this project. Surprise your child with a book that you create, then invite her to make one of her own.

☞ **What You Need:**

Paper, scissors, ruler, stickers or pictures, glue, pen or colored markers, hole punch, yarn

✄ **To Prepare:**

1. Choose a set of interesting stickers or pictures.

2. Cut 3- by 5-inch (or other size) papers for pages. Punch two holes in the short side of the pages and tie them together with bright yarn.

3. Apply a sticker or glue on a picture, then write a rhyme on each page.

☆ **Activity:**

Invite your child to read the book and add it to her library.

Examples:

- Picture: frog
  Sentences: I see a frog. A frog sees me. I swat a fly, but he eats three!

- Picture: flower and bee
  Sentences: The smell of pollen calls the bee. The bee makes honey for you and me.

- Picture: kitten
  Sentences: Muffin is my kitten's name. We run and jump and play a game.

- Picture: heart
  Sentences: A Valentine for you. A Valentine for me. A Valentine for baby, and that makes three.

- Picture: snowman
  Sentences: Spring is coming! The bluebirds are here. The snowman is melting. We'll see him next year.

- Picture: skyscraper
  Sentences: Great, tall building, you seem to touch the sky. The people who are in you can see the clouds go by.

- Picture: shoes
  Sentences: I need these as I cross the street so pebbles and twigs don't hurt my feet.

- Picture: helicopter
  Sentences: I have no wings and yet I fly. You'll see two rotors on me as I go by.

- Picture: apple with worm
  Sentences: Apple sweet and apple red. For a little worm, it is his bed.

- Picture: cookie
  Sentences: Blend butter and sugar, along with an egg. Then add some vanilla and a pinch of nutmeg. Pour in some flour, now beat, beat, beat. Bake it in the oven for a tasty treat!

- Picture: snowflake
  Sentences: I catch a snowflake on my hand. I hope that it will stay. But as I watch its pretty shape, it slowly melts away.

❧ 63 ❧

CURSIVE WRITING

This activity introduces cursive letters. To make the work extra special, give your child a new lined notebook* and pen or pencil. Tell him to try his best but not to erase mistakes. Explain that with a bit of effort he will soon become comfortable with this new way of writing.

> **This notebook will become his Spelling Notebook (Lesson 68), where he continues cursive practice with spelling words.*

☞ **What You Need:**
Wide-ruled, spiral-bound notebook (or lined paper); pen or pencil

☆ **Activity 1: Introducing the Lowercase Cursive Letters**
Introduce three new letters a day. If that is too many, do one or two. For each one, demonstrate how to write it, then have him practice the single letter, a two-letter combination, and then a word (see the next two pages).

1. On the first day, give your child the notebook and pen or pencil. Explain that you are going to show him a new way of writing, called cursive, which connects letters together smoothly and quickly. It is perfect for jotting notes and writing birthday, thank you, and holiday cards. He will also use cursive to sign his name on letters and official documents.

2. Tilt the paper to the left for right-handers and to the right for left-handers. Demonstrate cursive by writing a few words. Point out how the letters slant slightly to the right, which is different from printed letters that sit straight up and down on the lines. Explain that every letter has a "tail" that connects it to the next one. Have him find the tail of the last letter of each word.

3. Explain that you will show him how to write three new letters daily, and that he will practice them in the notebook. In a little over a week he will know how to write all the cursive letters.

4. With your child watching, write the cursive letter *a* several times in his notebook. Let him copy it as many times as he likes. Remind him to slant the letter to the right.

5. Now repeat with the cursive letter *b*. Next, write two connected *b*'s *(bb)* and have him do the same. Lastly, write a connected *b* and *a (ba)* and ask him to copy the pair.

6. For the final letter of the day, write the letter *c* and have him copy it several times. Practice *ca* together. Demonstrate and have him write *cab*.

7. Continue working through the alphabet, in subsequent lessons, introducing new letters using steps 4–6.

a b c d e f g h i j k l m n

o p q r s t u v w x y z

Examples:

This program is designed to introduce the cursive letters gradually, with repetition of those previously learned. Here's how his notebook might develop:

• a, a, a	a, a, a	a, a, a
• b, b, b	bb, bb, bb	ba, ba, ba
• c, c, c	ca, ca, ca	cab, cab, cab
• d, d, d	da, da, da	dad, dad, dad
• e, e, e	ea, ea, ea	bead, bead, bead

- f, f, f   fe, fe, fe   feed, feed, feed
- g, g, g   ga, ga, ga   gab, gab, gab
- h, h, h   he, he, he   hedge, hedge, hedge
- i, i, i   id, id, id   idea, idea, idea
- j, j, j   ji, ji, ji   jig, jig, jig
- k, k, k   ki, ki, ki   kid, kid, kid
- l, l, l   le, le, le   leak, leak, leak
- m, m, m   ma, ma, ma   mail, mail, mail
- n, n, n   ne, ne, ne   neck, neck, neck
- o, o, o   oi, oi, oi   oink, oink, oink
- p, p, p   po, po, po   police, police, police
- q, q, q   qu, qu, qu   quill, quill, quill
- r, r, r   ra, ra, ra   raining, raining, raining
- s, s, s   sh, sh, sh   shimmer, shimmer, shimmer
- t, t, t   tr, tr, tr   tropical, tropical, tropical
- u, u, u   um, um, um   umbrella, umbrella, umbrella
- v, v, v   vi, vi, vi   vitamin, vitamin, vitamin
- w, w, w   we, we, we   western, western, western
- x, x, x   ex, ex, ex   excuse, excuse, excuse
- y, y, y   ye, ye, ye   yellow, yellow, yellow
- z, z, z   zo, zo, zo   zoology, zoology, zoology

☆ Activity 2: Introducing the Capital Cursive Letters

Once your child is comfortable reading and writing the lowercase cursive letters, continue work in his notebook by introducing three cursive capital letters daily. Beginning with *A,* demonstrate how to write the capital letter, then have him practice it several times. Ask him to find two words that begin with that capital letter, for example, the name of a person, *Alice,* and the name of a place, *Atlanta.* Have him write each word two times. Continue this pattern with each of the capitals.

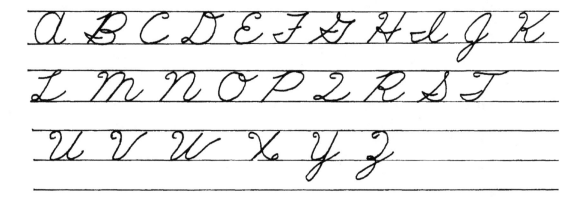

Note: Capital Q is shown above as it has been taught for many years, rather like the number 2. Now, however, some cursive styles present it as a larger version of its manuscript form: a large circle with a little tail added at the lower right. Search "cursive Q capital" online to view examples, then choose which you prefer to teach.

To find additional resources, search online for free cursive writing paper with dotted letter templates that you can print out.

Rules for Capitalization:

Review these three general rules with your child. Refer to the examples when capitalization questions arise.

1. Capitalize the first word of a sentence.

2. Capitalize proper nouns and proper adjectives such as these:

- Names and titles of people, races, nationalities, languages, and places: Amy Smith, Dr. Lang, Professor Kate Mills, President John Adams, Italian, New Yorker, Spanish olives, Lincoln National Monument, Los Angeles, Palm Beach, Japan, Willow Creek, Moose Mountain

- Organizations, companies, and products: Texas State University, Elmville Public Library, Martin's Skating Rink, the House of Representatives, Windy Mountain Gazette, Pepsi, Kleenex, Ford Explorer, Wheat Chex cereal, Whiskas cat food, Welsh's Grape Juice Cocktail

- Specific courses of study: Music 101, The History of Lollipops (General course names are not capitalized: I enjoy math, but Math 6 was difficult.)

- Names of days, months, and holidays: Monday, June, Mother's Day, Easter, Ramada, Hanukkah, Halloween (The seasons spring, summer, autumn, and winter are not capitalized.)

- Religious terms: God, Allah, Bible, Torah, Koran, Judaism, Islam, Christian, Hindu, Buddhist

- Abbreviations: 800 B.C., KPRK radio, FAA (Federal Aviation Administration), U.S.A. (United States of America)

3. Capitalize first, last, and important words in titles. Prepositions of four letters or less (of, for, with, on, by, in), conjunctions (and, or, but, so), and articles (a, an, the), are usually not capitalized unless they are the first word of the title:

- Books: The Hobbit

- Movies: The Wizard of Oz

- Plays: Jack and the Beanstalk

- Songs: "A Tree in the Wood"

- Poems: "The Fisherman"

- Articles: "Five Steps to Successfully (and Safely) Give Your Cat a Bath"

❧ 64 ❧

HOW TO WRITE A PARAGRAPH

Once your child can write sentences, show her how to arrange them into paragraphs. A paragraph should have at least three sentences: The first is called the topic sentence. Inner ones support, explain, or give more detail about the opening statement. The last sentence summarizes and restates the main idea or an important detail from the paragraph.

☞ **What You Need:**
Lined paper, pencil, old fashioned three-minute egg timer (optional)

☆ **Activity:**
Have your child follow these steps:

1. Write a topic sentence.

2. Write several sentences that develop the subject. Choose one of these methods:

   • Give details and information about the topic.

   • Offer examples of what you mean.

   • Support your topic sentence with reasons. Begin with your strongest argument and list them in order of importance.

   • Tell a story that helps your reader understand your point. Write in chronological order.

Example:

1. Give your child an object, a candle for example. Ask her to write one sentence, such as, "Mom set a candle on the table." If she tends to procrastinate, set an old fashioned three-minute egg timer on the table and challenge her to finish before the sand runs out.

2. Congratulate her, then ask her to write another sentence describing the candle. Again use the egg timer, if needed. She might write, "It is tall and white."

3. Again praise her. Invite her to write a sentence with either more description or that explains how the candle is used. For example, "Mom can light it with a match," or "It makes me think of my birthday," or "It smells like vanilla."

4. For the final sentence, ask her to conclude with a comment on what she thinks of the candle. For example, "I'm glad Mom brought me the candle," or "I like watching the flame."

5. Give her a hug and tell her that she just wrote a paragraph. Suggest she draw a picture to illustrate the page.

> My Pencil
> A pencil is my favorite tool. I use it to write stories and draw pictures of things I think about. With my pencil, I can draw pictures of dragons, cats, talking frogs, and frolicking elves. I can share with you my story about a trip to the moon. Truly, my pencil is an amazing tool!

Variation:

Another way to write a paragraph is to compare two things. These explanatory paragraphs contrast the likenesses and differences between two or more persons, places, things, or ideas. Begin with one point of view, then contrast it with another.

STORY TREE

Youngsters love surprises. Create a Story Tree one night and let your child discover it in the morning.

☞ What You Need:

Construction paper, writing paper, clear contact paper, pencil, colored marker, scissors, tape, hole punch, yarn

✂ To Prepare:

1. Cut a tree out of green construction paper. (For a large tree, piece together several sheets.) Cover it with clear contact paper and attach it to a bulletin board or wall.

2. Cut out five to ten colorful construction paper fruit shapes, such as a pear, banana, lemon, peach, pineapple, strawberry, and a bunch of grapes. Attach them to the tree with bits of double-sided tape.

3. Prepare a blank book. Assemble the same number of construction paper pages as pieces of fruit. Punch holes down the sides and bind with yarn. Write "Fruit Stories" on the cover with colored marker.

4. Cut sheets of writing paper to fit comfortably on the pages.

☆ **Activity:**

1. Invite your child to pluck a fruit from the tree. Give him a piece of pre-pared writing paper and ask him to craft a short story that includes the fruit in some way.

2. Have him open the book and glue his writing onto the right-hand page, then glue the fruit onto the facing page (back of the front cover).

3. Encourage him to write a new fruit story daily until the tree is empty.

Variation:

Instead of fruit, use pictures of things that interest your child, such as rockets, athletes, horses, jewelry, or mushrooms—or use an assortment of items.

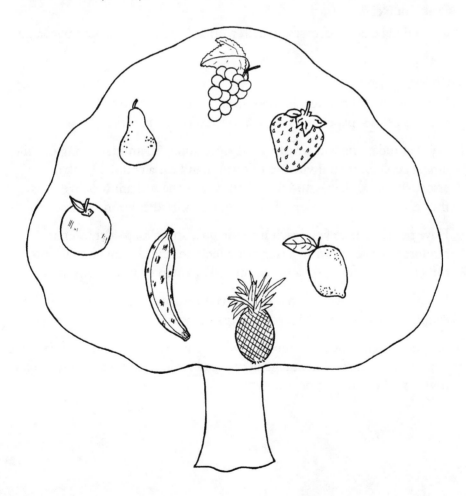

❧ 66 ❧

ANIMAL CRACKER STORIES

Let cute animal crackers inspire your child to write an imaginative story. Best of all, she gets to eat the cookies!

☞ **What You Need:**

Box of animal cracker cookies, pencil, writing paper, construction paper, glue

☆ **Activity:**

1. Keep the animal crackers hidden until it is time for the activity. Ask your child to get her paper and pencil and wait for the surprise.

2. Say that today she will write a short story about an animal. Bring out the box of cookies, then invite her to open it and eat a couple. Look at the assorted animal shapes and talk about where the real animals live, what they eat, and how they are adapted to their varied environments.

3. Have her close her eyes, reach into the box, and choose a cracker at random. Ask her to write a story that includes the chosen animal. It is sometimes helpful to set a time limit, such as ten or fifteen minutes.

4. When she is finished, ask her to read you the story. Invite her to eat a couple more crackers while you discuss her work.

5. Suggest she glue the story onto a piece of construction paper and decorate around the borders. Encourage her to read it aloud to friends and display it on a wall or bulletin board.

Variation 1:
Invite your child to take several animals from the box and include them in a story.

Variation 2:
Save the box when it is empty. Write full or partial topic sentences about jungle or zoo animals on slips of paper and place them in the box. Ask your child to choose a slip, copy the sentence or phrase on notebook paper, and then finish the story.

Examples:

- My African safari brought more adventure and excitement than I hoped for. . . .

- We cut our way through the thick vines and leaves until we came face to face with a . . .

- The circus monkey leaped out of the ring and onto my shoulder! Then . . .

- I did not realized how useful an elephant's trunk is until I saw it . . .

- My brother and I peered into the cave and were amazed to see . . .

- I knew that my parents had a special birthday surprise for me, but I never expected . . .

- Each night the _____ quietly came to her window. . . .

- Write about what people would say if you rode a giraffe into town.

- Choose two animals and compare their teeth. How are they different? How do they help each animal?

PERSONAL NOTES

Handwritten notes are like secret codes, a bit mysterious and always special. Your child loves getting messages written just for him. So, sometimes—instead of telling him something— jot down your statement or question on a piece of paper. Try playing a Silent Game, in which you agree on a time period during which you communicate only by writing. Another playful idea is to slip notes back and forth under a closed door.

Rosa
As soon as you read the
book, we will go to the library.
Tell me when you are
finished.   ♡ mom

John
You did a great
job making your
bed.

~

Please feed the
dog at 4:00.

Thanks ~ Dad

SPELLING NOTEBOOK

We learn to spell by reading and writing, and by thinking about how words are built. Here's a simple way to give your child consistent spelling practice and encourage independent writing. In addition, it gives effective cursive practice, eliminating the need for separate handwriting drills.

☞ **What You Need:**

Wide-ruled, spiral-bound notebook (use the notebook introduced in Cursive Writing, page 221, or start a new one), colored pens, lead pencil

✄ **To Prepare:**

Make one page at a time, as needed, using words associated with special interests, topics of study, or a theme—such as the following: fruit, airplanes, nuts, sewing, tools, kitchen utensils, sports, games, weather, gardening, animals, government, anatomy, transportation, clothing, shopping, minerals, flowers, the solar system, fish, states, a birthday party, art, music, toys, science, dinosaurs, breakfast foods, furniture, seasonal or holiday words.

1. Prepare a page in the Spelling Notebook by writing in cursive a list of ten words gathered from a dictionary, articles, or books. Include a few words from your child's current work that he finds hard to spell. (For younger children, use fewer words and print them.) For variety, write lists with pens of assorted colors.

2. Under the list of words, write a sentence for your child to copy. It does not have to include the vocabulary words. Leave space at the bottom for her to write a sentence of her own invention.

☆ **Activity:**

Introduce a new set of words weekly. Have your child do the following, using lead pencil for the writing portion:

1. Write the date at the top of the page.

2. For each word:

   • Say it aloud.

   • Spell it aloud.

   • With eyes closed, say the word, then spell it aloud.

   • Write the word three times.

3. Copy the sentence.

4. Write a sentence of her own.

Review her work. Have her correct any misspelled words and rewrite them three times. Include the spelling words in other lessons that week.

basil

← write date

oragano

thyme

rosemary

write each
word three
times

sage

parsley

savory

dill

fennel

tarragon

Toss the potatoes with olive oil,
garlic, and chives.

Copy sentence
once.

Child writes
own sentence.

Rewrite any
misspelled
words.

✌ 69 ✌

SPELLING JUMBLES

Solving these little word puzzles is a fun way to offer additional spelling practice.

☞ **What You Need:**
Small Letter Cards (page 118), muffin tin or egg carton

✂ **To Prepare:**
Choose five to twelve words that your child is familiar with. Prepare Spelling Jumbles by putting the Small Letter Cards for each word in the cups of a muffin tin or egg carton.

☆ **Activity:**
Demonstrate how to lay out one set of letters, at random, then arrange them into a word. Invite your child to continue building words, one at a time, placing them in a vertical row as they are completed.

Variation:
Add an extra letter to each cup. Tell your child that an unneeded letter has been added to each set. Ask him to build the words and place the extra letters to the side.

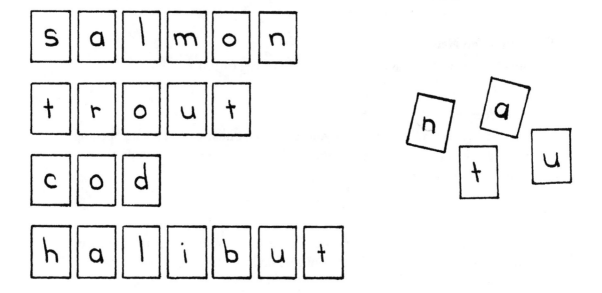

❧ 70 ❧

SPELLING CARDS

Use this collection of activities in conjunction with Spelling Notebook to help your child improve her spelling skills. Activity 1 introduces the basic lesson, which relies on word lists that you provide. Activities 2–6 are supplemental games to help her remember the words; alternate between them as you work with new sets of Spelling Cards. Occasionally review old sets of words so they are not forgotten.

☞ **What You Need:**

Colored cardstock or construction paper, scissors, ruler, pencil, colored markers, spelling words (assembled according to your child's needs), Spelling Notebook (page 234) or lined paper

Activity 6 requires either envelopes, a muffin tin, or an egg carton for storage purposes.

✂ **To Prepare:**

1. To make Spelling Cards, cut colored cardstock or construction paper into word-sized rectangles.

2. Write one word on each Spelling Card. A set of eight to ten cards is a good number to work with at one time.

Variation:

Instead of preparing the Spelling Cards for your child, give her a list of words and have her write them on the cards herself.

☆ Activity 1: Say and Write

1. Show your child the set of Spelling Cards and ask her to say the words. Make sure she understands what they mean.

2. Instruct her to follow these steps three times for each word:

   a. Say the word, for example, *"pumpkin."*

   b. Spell it aloud, *"p, u, m, p, k, i, n,"* without looking at the text.

   c. Write the word in her Spelling Notebook.

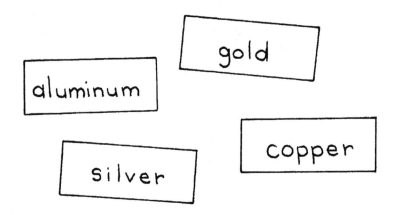

☆ Activity 2: Invent a Sentence

1. Shuffle the cards and place them face down.

2. Invite your child to choose one or more cards. Ask her to read the word(s) silently. Have her write a sentence using her selection(s).

3. Instruct her to continue choosing cards and writing sentences until all the cards are used.

4. Have her read the sentences to you, then congratulate her on a job well done!

☆ Activity 3: Spell It!

Hold the set of Spelling Cards facing you. Read the word on one card and ask your child to repeat the word and spell it aloud. Continue through the set. If she has trouble spelling a word verbally, have her try writing it.

☆ Activity 4: Alphabetize

Have your child arrange the Spelling Cards in alphabetical order. She could write the words in order, if desired.

☆ Activity 5: Dictionary Race

Each person needs a dictionary for this activity, which works well with two or more people.

1. Shuffle the Spelling Cards and place them face down.

2. One person turns over a card to show the word, then each player races to find the word in her dictionary. The first one to find it reads the definition aloud.

3. Repeat with the remaining Spelling Cards.

Variation:

To adapt the activity for one student, say a Spelling Cards word and ask her to find it as quickly as possible in a dictionary, then read you the definition. Repeat with the remaining cards.

☆ Activity 6: Puzzle Words

1. Have your child copy the words onto a new set of cards, leaving a space between each letter.

2. Tell her to cut each card to divide the letters. This makes Puzzle Words. Mix the letters of each Puzzle Word and keep them in separate piles.

3. Ask her to arrange the letters to rebuild each Puzzle Word, spelling aloud as she constructs them. She may enjoy racing against an old fashioned three-minute egg timer (the kind where falling sand tracks the time).

4. Store the Puzzle Words in separate envelopes, in a muffin tin, or in an egg carton until they are no longer needed.

❧ 71 ❧

CONTRACTIONS BOOK

Combine two words, remove one or more letters, replace them with an apostrophe, and you have a contraction. Your child has read contractions; now he will write them. Instead of making a separate Contractions Book, the project could also be written directly into his Spelling Notebook.

☞ What You Need:

Small Letter Cards (page 118), writing paper (or Spelling Notebook, page 234), pencil, colored pencil, scissors, hole punch, yarn; white or colored copy paper and glue (optional)

✄ To Prepare:

If using the Spelling Notebook, ignore these preparations and simply have your child write directly into the notepad.

Make pages for a Contractions Book by cutting writing paper into halves or quarters. To give each page more thickness, your child will glue the writing paper onto white or colored copy paper after he has completed it.

☆ Activity:

1. Have your child build *can not* with the Small Letter Cards.

2. Take away the letters *n* and *o,* and replace them with an apostrophe (use the *comma* Small Letter Card). Scoot the remaining letters together to form the word *can't.* Explain that the apostrophe tells us where letters are missing. Together, say a few sentences using *can not* and *can't.*

3. Ask him to write *can not = can't* on the top line of the prepared paper, using lead pencil for all the words except the contraction *can't,* which he writes with colored pencil.

4. On the next line(s), he writes a sentence that uses the words *can not,* for example, "The dog *can not* leave the yard."

5. On the next line(s), he writes the sentence a second time, this time using the contraction, "The dog *can't* leave the yard." Have him write the contraction with the same colored pencil that he used to write it at the top of the page. If he is bored by rewriting the same sentence, suggest he change the second one. It should, however, stay with the same subject, for example: "The dog can't jump over the fence," "It can't read a book," or "The dog can't see the rabbit."

6. Repeat steps 1–5 for other contractions (next page). If he is working on loose pages (instead of the Spelling Notebook), save the sheets and have him glue them (lightly around the edges) onto the copy paper. When all the pages are completed, punch holes down the side and bind with yarn.

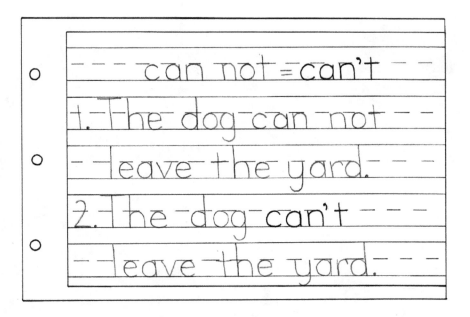

Examples:

Here are some contractions that your child should know:

- do not: don't
- are not: aren't
- would not: wouldn't
- could not: couldn't
- should not: shouldn't
- will not: won't
- they will: they'll
- we will: we'll
- he will: he'll
- we will: we'll
- they have: they've
- you have: you've
- I have: I've
- is not: isn't
- can not: can't
- you would: you'd
- you will: you'll
- I will: I'll
- she will: she'll
- I would: I'd

PART 5

CREATIVE READING
& WRITING

By now, your child has a good understanding of basic reading and writing. Building on those skills simply requires daily practice. It doesn't matter what curriculum—if any—you follow, as long as he reads from a variety of materials and writes about subjects that interest him.

Your goal is to teach him how to write clearly so he can convey his thoughts to others. Encourage him to read what he has written aloud to discover any missing words and see if it makes sense. Find ways to keep activities enjoyable by linking projects to subjects he finds engaging and by keeping assignments short. It is better that he writes a little bit each day with enthusiasm than for him to sit staring at a sheet of paper, hating every moment of work.

This section is full of playful ideas to help you with this task. Is your child very active? Then try Lesson 72: Spin, Point, and Write to get his creativity flowing. Is he quiet and thoughtful? Give Lesson 74: Mystery Object a try. Sticker-happy children will love Lesson 77: Sticker Stories. Adventure-loving kids will delight in making Lesson 82: Treasure Map. And there are many more ideas for you to explore!

ༀ 72 ༀ

PARAGRAPH JUMBLES

This lesson helps your child think logically as she puts sentences in order. Begin by building short, simple paragraphs, then progress to longer, more complex ones.

☞ What You Need:

Lined paper, pencil or pen, scissors, paper clips, basket or box

✂ To Prepare:

1. Invent a paragraph or find one in a book. Make sure it has a strong topic sentence and an obvious order from the first to last sentence.

2. Write the paragraph on lined paper. Begin each sentence on a new line and leave a space below, as shown.

3. Cut the sentences apart and shuffle them. Secure the set of sentence strips with a paper clip to make a Paragraph Jumble.

4. Repeat steps 1–3 with other paragraphs to make additional Paragraph Jumbles. Place them in a pretty container.

☆ Activity:

1. Present your child with a Paragraph Jumble. Invite her to set out the sentence strips at random.

2. Have her read each strip, then find the "topic sentence" that is the logical beginning to the paragraph. Set that strip at the top of the work space.

3. Have her read the remaining sentences and place them in sequential order.

4. Once the entire paragraph is built, ask her to read it aloud. Does it make sense?

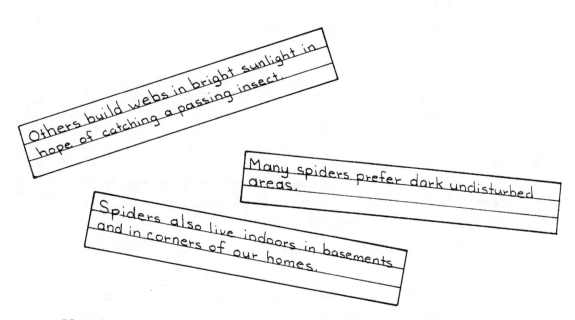

Spiders live in many parts of the earth.

You can find them in forests, deserts, seashores, and in your backyard.

Others build webs in bright sunlight in hope of catching a passing insect.

Many spiders prefer dark undisturbed areas.

Spiders also live indoors in basements and in corners of our homes.

Variation:

Add one or two sentences that don't belong with the paragraph. These could be topic sentences that obviously refer to another subject. Tell your child to look for them and set them side.

✣ 73 ✣

MYSTERY OBJECT

Try this nifty exercise to enliven the day's writing assignment. Don't worry about misspelled words; for this lesson you want your child to express himself without being inhibited by thoughts of "making a mistake."

☞ What You Need:
A cloth or paper bag, assortment of varied-textured items (button, feather, pencil, walnut, small toy, etc), lined writing paper, pencil

✂ To Prepare:
Place an item into the bag. To preserve the mystery, make sure your child doesn't see you do this.

☆ Activity:
1. Tell your child that you have placed a mystery object in the bag and that he will feel the item and write down his impressions. Explain that he must stay silent and communicate only in writing.

2. Have him begin by simply touching the object, withdrawing his hand, and then recording his first impressions.

3. Ask him to feel it a second time and jot down what comes to mind. Continue this several more times.

4. Finally, have him write down his guess of what the item is, then open the bag and look.

Variation:

Conclude the above activity by asking your child to rewrite his impressions into a descriptive paragraph. Have him draw the object at the top of a sheet of paper and attach the paragraph below, as shown.

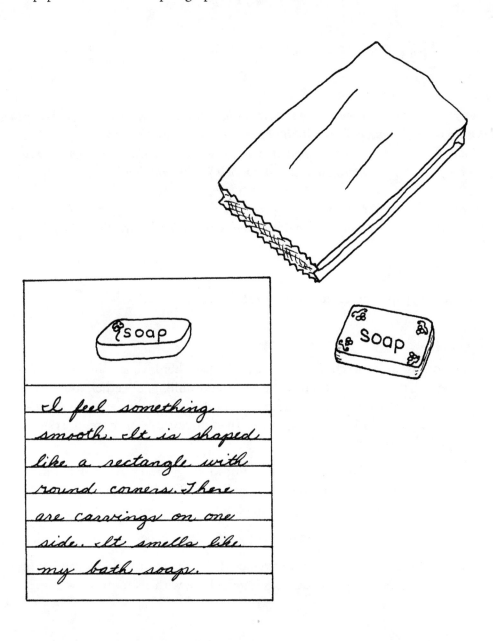

74

HOW TO WRITE A LETTER

In this age of instant communication, there is still something special about a handwritten letter. Preparing a notecard takes a bit of effort, but a few well-chosen words can brighten a friend's day. For the recipient, knowing that the sender took the time to choose and write the postcard, letter, or notecard adds to their joy in receiving it.

Keep this tradition alive by encouraging your child to acknowledge gifts and thoughtful actions with thank you notes and to correspond with a friend or relative by mail.

☞ **What You Need:**

Lined notepaper, notecard, or postcard; pencil

☆ **Activity:**

1. Before asking your child to write a letter, have her imagine the recipient opening the mailbox, finding the letter, and smiling. Together, look at a sample note, as illustrated, and point out the important parts: date, salutation, body, closing, and signature. Then discuss one or more ideas she would like to include in her message.

2. Have her write the letter once, to set down its general form. Ask her to read the sentences aloud to see if they flow smoothly and make sense. Check the spelling and have her make any changes.

3. Now instruct her write the final copy onto lined paper or in a notecard.

4. Show her how to address the envelope, write the return address, and affix the stamp. She may enjoy decorating the back with a sticker or two.

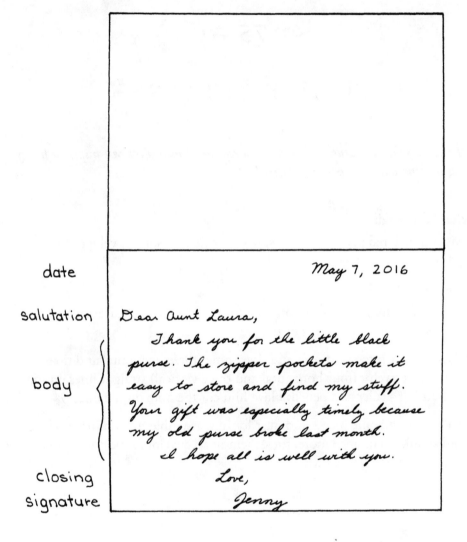

date — May 7, 2016

salutation — Dear Aunt Laura,

body — Thank you for the little black purse. The zipper pockets make it easy to store and find my stuff. Your gift was especially timely because my old purse broke last month.
I hope all is well with you.

closing — Love,

signature — Jenny

Variation:

Postcards come in a variety of fascinating pictures and designs. Because of their small size, your child may find writing on them less intimidating—and more fun—than crafting a letter. The next time you are shopping, invite her to choose postcards for several friends, then encourage her to write a few sentences on each and send them off.

PUZZLE LETTERS

Puzzle Letters are fun to make and exciting to receive. This project can inspire a flurry of pen pal writing with a friend or relative.

☞ **What You Need:**

Cardstock, colored pens or markers, pencil, ruler, scissors, envelope

☆ **Activity:**

1. Invite your child to write a note to a friend on a piece of cardstock. Suggest he use colored pens or markers.

2. Have him turn the card over and draw nine (three horizontal and three vertical) or twelve (four horizontal and three vertical) straight lines on the back, using a ruler and pencil. Have him cut the note on the lines.

3. Ask him to mix the pieces and, just for fun, assemble them himself. Have him shuffle them once more, tuck them in an envelope, and then give or mail the note to a friend.

STICKER STORIES

A set of imaginative stickers adds an element of fun to story writing!

☞ **What You Need:**

Assorted stickers, writing paper, pencil

☆ **Activity:**

Give your child a sheet of writing paper, a pencil, and a sheet of unusual or amusing stickers. Invite her to write a story, using the stickers in place of some words.

Sammy the 🐜 fell into a hole in the sand. Soon, a 🐞 came by and asked Sammy 🐜 if he needed help. The 🐞 crawled down to help the 🐜. The 🐞 and the 🐜 were both stuck! A 🦟 flew over and...

Variation:

Use holiday stickers to spark your child's imagination and inspire her to write stories, poems, or comics.

✑ 77 ✑

SPIN, POINT, AND WRITE

"But I can't think of anything to write about!" your child moans. Suggest he try this activity to discover subjects for a unique story.

☞ **What You Need:**

Writing paper, pencil

☆ **Activity:**

1. Tell your child to choose a room or a place outdoors. Have him close his eyes and spin around a few times, then stop, raise his arm, and point straight ahead. Have him open his eyes and name what he is pointing at.

2. That item become the subject for his writing project.

Variation:

Suggest he spin three times to find three things to include in his story.

Jack-O-Lantern Stories

Here's a holiday-inspired creative writing idea that you can easily adapt to fit other special occasions.

☞ **What You Need:**

Small hollow plastic Jack-O-Lantern, construction paper, scissors, pen

✄ **To Prepare:**

1. Cut a piece of construction paper into the shape shown on the next page and write, "Reach inside me, I won't bite. Find a story you can write." Tape it to the back of the Jack-O-Lantern so it sticks up.

2. Write story suggestions on slips of orange paper and tuck them into the Jack-O-Lantern.

Examples:

- The laughing ghost
- Uncle Bruce's Jack-O-Lantern
- The Jack-O-Lantern that came alive
- Kitty's pumpkin patch
- The smallest pumpkin
- The pumpkin that couldn't stop growing!
- Samuel chooses a pumpkin.

- Mr. Scarecrow tells his story.

- A "batty" story

- Aunt Abigail's yummy pumpkin pie

☆ **Activity:**

1. Introduce the Jack-O-Lantern. Invite your child to pull out a slip and write a story on the suggested topic.

2. Encourage her to decorate the story with a picture or holiday stickers.

Variation 1:

Invite your child to write a short story daily for one week. When finished, add a construction paper cover, punch holes down the side, and bind with yarn. Let her decorate the cover creatively.

Variation 2:

Have her write a story on lined paper. Cut it out and glue it onto black paper. Decorate the edges with pumpkin stickers or construction paper cutouts and display on a wall or bulletin board.

✣ 79 ✣

THE BOO BOOK!

Give your child's sense of humor free expression with this Halloween project. Use this idea for any set of holiday stickers or pictures.

☞ What You Need:
Orange construction paper, Halloween stickers, scissors, stapler, colored markers

✂ To Prepare:
Cut orange construction paper into quarters.

☆ Activity:
1. Invite your child to put a Jack-O-Lantern or other holiday sticker on a quarter piece of construction paper.

2. Ask him to write a cartoon caption for the picture, adding art of his own. Repeat for the remaining three (or more) pages.

3. When all the pages are completed, staple them together and title it "The Boo Book!"

4. Encourage him to share the book with friends and add it to his library.

HOLIDAY CARD STORIES

Holiday cards have beautiful pictures that invite the creation of a story. Let your child choose his favorite cards, daydream about the scenes, and then write stories based on them. Once several are completed, he can create his own Holiday Book. Store the book with seasonal decorations so your family can enjoy reading it every year.

☞ What You Need:

Holiday cards, construction paper, lined writing paper, scissors, pen

☆ Activity:

Have your child follow these steps:

1. Choose a holiday card, close her eyes and imagine what it would feel like to actually be in the scene.

2. On lined paper, write a story, poem, or description inspired by the card.

3. Glue the card and story onto construction paper.

4. Display the completed piece and read it to the family.

Encourage your child to write a collection of short stories over a period of days or weeks. Form them into a book by adding a decorative construction paper cover, punching holes down the side, and binding with yarn. The illustration shows a story our son wrote when he was nine years old.

Christmas

It's Christmas Eve and the father is anxious to get home before Christmas. "I hope the train will be on time," the father said. When he heard the train's whistle he looked and it was there. On the train the father thought, "Well, I'll be on time! Let me see, in one box there's a BB gun for Tommy and in the other box there is a stuffed cat for Sue!" Finally he got home and said to Tommy and Sue, "Go put the presents under the tree!" On Christmas, the children ran to the tree and opened the presents. "Oh thank you, thank you," they cried.

~ 81 ~

SHORT STORY IDEAS

Try these ideas to encourage creative writing. Note misspelled words and incorporate them into your child's Spelling Notebook (page 234), but don't stifle his process by pointing them out at this time. Praise his efforts and encourage him to continue jotting down stories. The more he reads and writes, the more his skills will improve.

☞ **What You Need:**

Lined paper, pencil

☆ **Activity:**

Invite your child to write about one of these topics:

- My Dream House: Describe what it would look like inside and out. What special features would it have?

- A Balloon Ride: What colors or designs are on the balloon? Where do you go? Who do you bring with you?

- Write three paragraphs about your family's car. In paragraph one tell why you like, dislike, or appreciate the car. In paragraph two, describe the car's exterior and interior. In paragraph three, tell where the car has traveled.

- My World: Write about life from your pet's perspective. Invent a pet if you don't have one.

- Cloud Pictures: Go outside and watch the clouds. Write a story inspired by their shapes.

- Write several paragraphs about an event with titles such as "A Bath for Rover," "My Dentist," "My Favorite Movie," "Popcorn Party," "Diving for Pennies," "An Afternoon with Aunt Julie," "The Haircut,"etc.

- Imagine you find a shipwreck on a beach. What happens next?

- My Star Ship: If you designed a spaceship for yourself, what would it look like and where would you go?

- The Storm: Tell about an extraordinary storm you experienced.

- Write about the funniest event you can remember.

- Choose a real or imaginary animal. Describe what it looks like, where it lives, how it spends its time, and its relationship with other animals.

- My Special Room: If you could design and decorate your room, what would it look like?

- Tell the story of a tree near your home. How old do you think it is? What creatures live in it? If it could see and speak, what might it say about what it has experienced?

- Pick a common item, such as a ball, spoon, yarn, or toothpick. Describe three ways in which it could be used in an unusual way.

- Choose one of your hobbies and explain how you do it, what you like about it, and what goals you hope to achieve with it.

- Describe a seasonal event, such as the first snow, autumn's entrance, the first flower you find in spring, or the abundance and warmth of summer.

- Read about your favorite movie star, singer, or athlete and find out how they trained for their job. Include him or her in a short story.

- Without naming it, describe your favorite food. Have other people read your description and guess what it is.

- Ask a grandparent or other adult about their childhood. How was it different from yours? Write down one of their stories.

- Rummage in a drawer to find an old coin or button. Write about where the item may have traveled and how it got to your home.

ॐ 82 ॐ

TREASURE MAP

Ahoy, mates! There's a tale to be told and gold to be found. This activity gives children who love adventure stories the opportunity to create a make-believe world of their own by writing directions and drawing a map to locate "hidden treasure."

The illustrations are based on a Treasure Map my son made years ago. The pirate feeling is unmistakable!

☞ **What You Need:**

White paper, pencil, dark tea or coffee, iron; match, lighter, or candle

☆ **Activity:**

Have your child follow these steps to make a Treasure Map. Supervise her use of the iron and flame.

1. On a piece of plain white paper, write the directions for finding pirate treasure. Leave at least a 1-inch border around the edge.

2. Draw a map to match your written directions.

3. Crumple the papers and soak them in a bowl of strong dark tea or coffee. Remove them from the liquid when brown, then flatten and let it dry. Optional: when the paper is almost dry, press it lightly with a cool iron. (Caution! Do this with adult supervision.)

4. With adult help, singe the edges of the papers with a match, lighter, or candle to make them look aged and pirate-like.

Go to the Black Sea and find the island Yalta. Then walk to Mount Tribble and climb to the crater. Look for the blackened stump. When you find it, kick it over and dig for treasure.

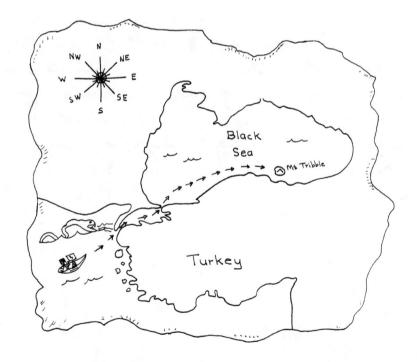

Variation:

Write a page from a pirate's diary.

Red Rackham's diary   Oct. 7, 1670

At high tide this morning, we boarded a freighter and took the loot and prisoners, sinking the brig by mid-morning. Share of loot is ten pounds of pieces of silver, fifty gold crowns, one princess's crown studded with jewels, and 90,000 pounds. Located with rest of loot. Map tells where it's hidden and how to find it. The rest of the day was peaceful with a fair wind at our sails. One whale sighted, gave chase but no success. 8:00 p.m. went to bed. Slept all night.

❧ 83 ❧

FAVORITE JOKES BOOK

This playful project gives your child the task of collecting jokes from friends and relatives, then writing them in a book of his own.

☞ **What You Need:**

Jokes, writing paper, pencil, construction paper or cardstock, hole punch, yarn

☆ **Activity:**

Have your child follow these directions:

1. Ask friends and relatives to tell you their favorite jokes.

2. Write the jokes on lined paper, giving each a title and attributing it to the person it came from.

3. Arrange the jokes on full-, half-, or quarter-sheets of construction paper or cardstock. Glue them in place and decorate, if desired.

4. Write "Favorite Jokes Book" on a construction paper cover. Punch holes down one side of the papers, then bind them with yarn.

Variation:

Ask participants to include pictures of themselves along with the jokes, then include those photos when making the book.

84

ONE-A-DAY STICKER STORIES

Give your child a set of special stickers or pictures on a subject that she adores. Challenge her to invent a little story about each one and watch her interest in writing soar.

☞ **What You Need:**

Lined paper, plain paper, pencil, stickers, glue, hole punch, yarn

✂ **To Prepare:**

1. Cut plain paper in half.

2. Cut lined paper to fit on the plain paper, as shown.

☆ **Activity:**

1. Show your child the special stickers. Invite her to choose one and write a few sentences—either a description or a story—about it. Encourage her to write quickly, so she doesn't get "stuck" on the project.

2. Ask her to read you her story, then glue it onto the plain paper and affix the sticker at the top.

3. Do one page daily or every few days, saving the work until the project is finished. Punch holes down one side of the pages, then bind with yarn to form a book.

Example:

Our daughter, Angela, loves cats. When she was eight years old we gave her a set of forty cute Victorian cat stickers, each dressed in a different outfit. Angela chose one sticker daily, gave the cat a name that became the title of the story, then wrote a few sentences describing its costume or activity.

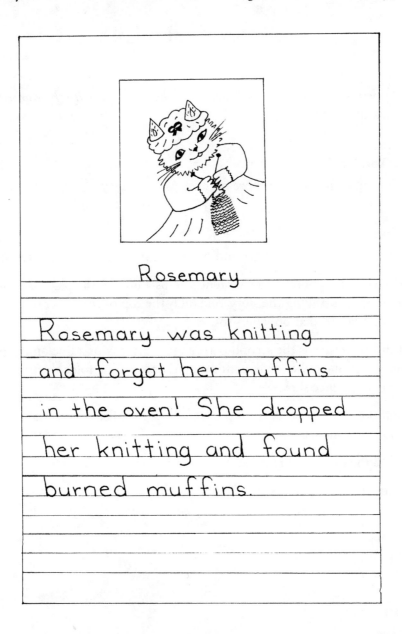

Rosemary

Rosemary was knitting and forgot her muffins in the oven! She dropped her knitting and found burned muffins.

85

STORY CHAINS

This activity gets the whole family writing. Build Story Chains with three or more people and expect lots of laughs.

☞ **What You Need:**

Lined paper, pencil, two or more friends

☆ **Activity:**

1. One person writes a sentence and passes the paper to a second person.

2. The second person reads the sentence, skips a line on the page, then writes a sentence continuing the story. She folds the top of the paper over the first sentence so that only hers shows.

3. A third player reads the second person's sentence, skips a line on the page, then writes one of her own, continuing the story. She folds the paper so only her sentence shows.

4. Continue until the story is finished, the paper is filled, or a certain amount of time has elapsed.

5. Unfold the paper and read the entire story aloud.

6. Optional: Draw a picture to illustrate the story.

There was a large castle on the hill.

A princess lived in the castle.

This was a tiny underwater castle.

A multitude of fish people lived in it.

Variation:

Pick one topic, such as elephants. Have each person write a sentence pertaining to elephants on a strip of paper. Mix up the strips and read them aloud to make a silly story.

86

POETRY

Check out children's poetry books from the library and read them with your child. Discuss what the poems mean and how the authors have carefully chosen the words to convey powerful images or emotions. Invite your child to create poems of her own. Many children—even some who dislike writing—enjoy expressing themselves through poetry. Here are some ideas to get you started.

☞ **What You Need:**

Lined paper, pencil

☆ **Activity 1:**

Write down the poems your child tells you. Form them into a little book she can share with friends.

☆ **Activity 2:**

Have her write down and illustrate her own poems. Again, form them into booklets.

☆ **Activity 3:**

Invite her draw a picture or assemble a collage of pictures that captures the feeling of an event, depicts the turning of the seasons, illustrates a holiday, or is descriptive of an item, pet, or person she admires. When the project is completed, have her write a poem about it.

☆ **Activity 4:**

Show her how to speak her own and other people's poems into a recording device. Make a recording of her poems, writings, songs, and thoughts once a year.

☆ **Activity 5:**

Fold a piece of construction paper in half or quarters to form a card. Have your child write her poem onto the card and send it to a relative or friend.

Examples:

Here are three poems written by our daughter, Angela. As you can see, poetry can be inspired by simple items or events that capture the imagination:

Wash
Swish! Swish! Swash! Swash!
Round and round goes the wash.
I open it up and take a look,
And notice somebody threw in a book!

Staring at the Ceiling
Staring at the ceiling, here I lie in bed,
I am very sick, or so the lady said.
She will often come, ask me how I'm feeling,
Then she will leave me, staring at the ceiling.

Staring at the ceiling, squashed spiders I do see,
Occasionally a live one, staring down at me.
Then she came again, said she was a'cleaning,
It was the spiders, that she was a'meaning.

Staring at the ceiling, now so white and clean,
Such a brand-new, shiny looking sheen.
Staring at the ceiling, nothing left to see,
Gone are the spiders, such good friends to me.

Wind
Inside, safe and sound,
Outside, fury bound.
Ripping at our safe retreat,
Biting, nipping at our feet,
Howling, howling all about,
Sounding like a giant's shout.
Huddled inside we do stay . . .
With hope the wind will go away.

Poetry doesn't have to rhyme. Thoughtful prose set down with carefully chosen words crosses the line from short story to poem. Our son, Christopher, wrote "The Pan Pipe" at the age of ten. He wrote it on binder paper, cut it out with scalloped edges, and glued it onto orange construction paper. Then he decorated around the edges by gluing on snips of red, orange, yellow, and green paper to represent fall leaves:

The Pan Pipe
Here comes autumn with a song on her lips and a dance on her feet. Merry is the forest with feasting and dancing.

The pan pipe plays about feasting and merry making while the fauns dance and sing under the blazing flame of the oak trees. The boughs of beech and rose trees ablaze hang over a table laden with good things to eat.

Now, autumn has come to an end and the pan pipe has stopped playing. The frost has come while we wait eagerly for the next sound of the pan pipe.

☆ **Activity 6:**
Read and write Japanese Haiku poems, which are built on this pattern: five syllables on the first line, seven syllables on the second line, five syllables on the last line.

Examples:

Here is a Haiku Christopher wrote:

Panther
In the wild wet woods,
Creeping stealthily along,
Panther springs unseen!

And here is one by Angela:

The Cat
Green eyes shining bright,
Wee mouse creeping in the night,
Pounce! Squeak! Then silence.

87

RECIPE BOOK

If your child enjoys cooking, invite him to make a personalized recipe book. He reads and writes while assembling his album of favorite dishes, then follows directions and measures ingredients while preparing the recipes. Best of all, he gets the satisfaction of eating the food he makes, as well as sharing it with others.

Preparing an entire meal makes an engaging project for a couple of older children. They can plan and write a menu, make decorations for the table, choose music to set the mood, seat guests, and serve the food. After all that work, it's nice if other members of the family contribute by cleaning up, but some children insist on completing the entire activity for themselves by restoring the kitchen to its original condition.

☞ **What You Need:**

Binder with section dividers and lined paper or large file box with cards in assorted colors; scissors, pencil, recipes (from cookbooks, online, or family collection), food ingredients

✂ **To Prepare:**

1. Discuss the project. Explain that beginning with a few recipes he can gradually build his collection to create a personalized Recipe Book.

2. Together, decide what form the Recipe Book will take: it could be in a sectioned binder filled with lined paper or in a file box with dividers (using colored cards for different categories). Alternately, it could be created in a computer database, but to give additional writing practice, the former two are preferable.

3. Once you have decided what format to follow, collect the materials and proceed with the Activity.

Example 1: Suggestions for a Simple Six-Section Recipe Book

Salads, Soups, Main Dishes, Desserts, Snacks, Other

Example 2: Another Way to Divide the Recipe Book

Breakfast, Lunch, Dinner, Snacks and Desserts

Example 3: Suggestions for a Sixteen-Section Recipe Book

Salads, Dressing and Sauces, Soups, Sandwiches and Spreads, Quick Breads, Yeast Breads, Main Dishes, Vegetables, Pasta, Rice, Beans and Tofu, Eggs, Meat and Fish, Desserts, Cookies, Other

---

Pancakes

1¼ cups flour	1 tablespoon sugar
1 teaspoon baking powder	1 egg
½ teaspoon soda	2 tablespoons oil
¼ teaspoon salt	1¼ cups buttermilk

Stir together dry ingredients. Beat wet ingredients, then stir in flour mixture. For each pancake, pour ¼ cup of batter into medium-hot skillet. May add blue-berries or chopped nuts to batter.

☆ **Activity:**

1. With your child, discuss the importance of eating a healthy, balanced diet that includes lots of fresh fruits and vegetables. Explain that a good cook prepares delicious meals using ingredients that nourish the body with nutrients it needs to function well.

2. Look at recipes in several cookbooks, then ask him to choose one that he likes. Begin with one that is a family favorite and that you know works well. Guide him to select a simple one to begin with so he isn't over-whelmed writing long lists of ingredients and complicated instructions.

3. Have him copy the recipe into his Recipe Book or onto a file card. Suggest he make it in the next day or two. Supervise and help where needed.

FAVORITE SUBJECT GUIDEBOOK

This project guides your child in making a booklet on a topic that intrigues her. Because it is built in a series of small steps, she isn't overwhelmed by the thought of writing a big report. She also learns to study independently. If she likes frogs, for example, she can make a Frog Guidebook. Each day she will read about a different kind of frog, draw it, and then write a few sentences describing its appearance, habitat, etc.

☞ **What You Need:**

Construction paper, lined writing paper, pictures or stickers of the guidebook subjects (or student can draw the pictures), reference material on the chosen subject (books, magazines, online articles), colored or lead writing pencils, scissors, glue, hole punch, yarn

✂ **To Prepare:**

1. Cut construction paper to make pages. Punch holes down the left side.

2. Cut writing paper to fit on the pages, as shown below.

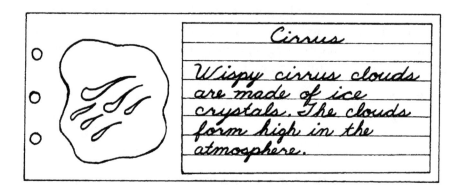

Examples:

Here are sample guidebook subjects. (Some, such as drinking vessels and hats, can lead to historical research to find types used in distant times):

• Cats	• Herbs	• Flowers
• Dogs	• Insects	• Tidepool Creatures
• Horses	• Planets	• Circus Animals
• Dinosaurs	• Rocks	• Clouds
• Fruit	• Seeds	• Egyptian Landmarks
• Amphibians	• Hats	• Medieval Weapons
• Flags	• Pasta	• Drinking Vessels
• Cars	• Birds	• Olympic athletes
• Composers	• Scientists	• Storybook Characters

☆ **Activity:**

1. Invite your child to read about the subject of her choice and select eight to ten varieties for her project.

2. Have her draw or attach a picture or sticker of the first item on the left side of a piece of prepared construction paper.

3. On the prepared writing paper, have her write one or more sentences describing the picture.

4. Ask her to glue her writing next to the picture.

5. Have her do the next page on another day. When eight to ten pages are finished, add a construction paper cover, punch holes down the side, and bind with yarn. Invite her to write a title on the book and decorate the cover. Add it to her library and encourage her to read it to friends.

Variation:

Younger children can make one-word guidebooks by having them write only the names of the pictures instead of sentences.

89

CROSSWORD PUZZLES

Crossword puzzles give extra spelling practice and help develop problem-solving skills. Choose words at random or focus on one topic in science, geography, sports, music, or other area.

☞ **What You Need:**

Paper, pen, list of words

✄ **To Prepare:**

1. Work out the puzzle by writing words crossword fashion, fitting them so they intersect.

2. Once you have a final design, draw squares for the crossword pattern on new paper.

3. On another sheet, write clues for each word.

☆ **Activity:**

Introduce your child to any words she may not be familiar with. Invite her to read the clues and fill in the puzzle.

Variation:

Suggest she make her own crossword. Here is one our daughter created on the topic of plants.

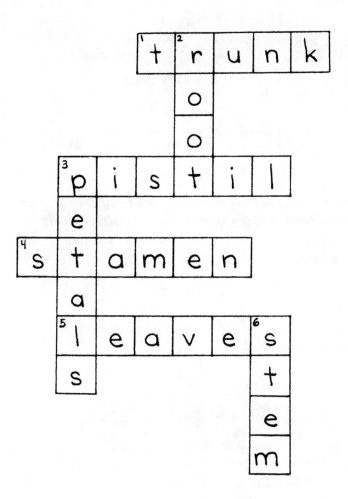

Across

1. Trees have a long ___.
3. There is one ___ inside
   a flower.
4. The ___ surround the
   pistil.
5. Plants have many
   green ___.

Down

2. The ___ is the underground
   part of a plant.
3. ___ are the pretty parts
   of a flower.
6. The ___ supports the
   flower.

90

DICTIONARY RACE

One, two, three, go! This game improves your child's skill at finding words in the dictionary. It also provides writing practice and improves his ability to put words in alphabetical order. Although there is a racing element, no points are kept, and by the end everyone is a winner.

☞ **What You Need:**

A dictionary for each player (from different publishers, if possible), paper, pencil or pen, scissors, basket

✂ **To Prepare:**

1. Cut a batch of one-word-sized slips of paper. Put them in a basket.

2. Choose a set of ten words drawn at random or from a current spelling list, favorite hobby, or subject of interest. Write them on ten prepared paper slips to make Word Cards and set aside.

☆ **Activity:**

1. Set out the basket of blank paper slips, along with pencils or pens.

2. Show a Word Card and say the word written on it. Players race to locate it in their dictionaries as quickly as possible. The first person to find it shouts, "Got it!" then quietly waits for the other player(s) to do so.

3. Each person reads his definition aloud. The one who finished first, reads first. (If using identical dictionaries, players take turns reading the definition on succeeding rounds.) Discuss the word's meaning and how it is described differently by different lexicographers (the authors or editors of a dictionary).

4. Each player takes a blank paper slip from the basket, writes the word on it, and then sets it aside.

5. Repeat steps 2–4 until all the words have been looked up and written.

6. Finally, ask players to arrange the words alphabetically in a vertical row, referring to the dictionary or reciting the alphabet if they need help remembering the proper order. Encourage children to help each other and discuss any problem words. When the activity is finished, congratulate all on a job well done.

Botanical Words	Painting Words
awn	canvas
calyx	carmine
conifer	easel
deciduous	ferrule
drupe	fresco
pistil	mural
rhizome	palette
stamen	portrait
tuber	tempera
umbel	turpentine

or

SECRET FRIENDS

If your child doesn't have a pen pal (or even if he does), consider creating a secret friend to inspire him to write in new and creative ways.

☞ **What You Need:**

Lined paper, pencil

☆ **Activity:**

Think about what excites your child and build a character on that theme. Write him a note based on that character and ask him to respond.

Examples:

I created pen pals for Angela and Christopher when they were eight and ten years old respectively. One morning, when they came downstairs, each found a letter from a mysterious pen pal. They eagerly wrote a response, and the next morning a new note was waiting in reply. Although several days would sometimes pass between messages, they enjoyed the personal attention and replied with enthusiasm. Now that they are adults, they remember their make-believe worlds fondly.

1. For Christopher, I created Taniff. Here is the first letter:

> Christopher,
>
> I am Taniff! I am a boy like you, but I do not live on Earth. I live on the planet VESTAR! I am curious about your planet and its strange customs, and I'm looking for a boy contact on Earth who will enlighten me.
>
> We have a special machine on Vestar, that I get to use sometimes, that allows me to ZAP things from my planet to yours—or the other way.
>
> Will you write to me? I promise that I will tell you all about my planet in exchange for your letters.
>
> I will answer when I can.
>
> Your friend,
>
> Taniff

This letter elicited a long reply (page-and-a-third of cursive writing on college-rule notebook paper). The pen pal relationship developed over the next five months until other interests took over.

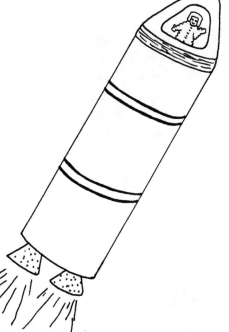

2. Angela loved cats, so it was only natural to create Mirabelle!

Dearest Angela,

I am a rather cute calico kitten, and I am writing to you from Catland!

I found a secret way to sneak into your world once in a while. Will you be my pen pal? I have been searching all over for someone who would understand me and share secrets about your world with me. In exchange, I'll tell you all about Catland, where I live.

If you write to me, I'll answer when I can slip into your world and snatch your note.

Fondly,

Mirabelle (signed with a drawn paw print)

My children sometimes included little items with their letters. Angela sent Mirabelle a piece of cheese—which doesn't exist in Catland—and Mirabelle told Angela all about mouseberries . . . a cat delicacy.

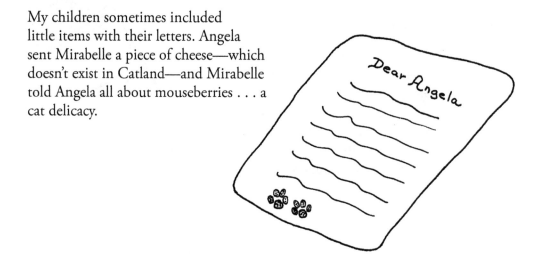

Think about what excites your child and create a pen pal of your own!

PART 6

LEARNING MORE ABOUT

LANGUAGE

In this section, you'll find suggestions on how to instruct your child to write book reports, articles on places, and biographies. These guides give structure to a sometimes puzzling process and help students organize information and their thoughts. Use these outlines to get your child started, then allow her creativity to personalize the work.

You'll also find ideas for setting up a reading club (Activity 93: Book Club). By creating a social group that values reading, you'll foster an environment where literacy is appreciated. The club also gives members practice summarizing books and expressing themselves clearly.

The final chapters introduce grammar—usually a rather dry subject—in a bright new way. Each part of speech (nouns, verbs, etc.) is carefully explained and linked to a rainbow color, then used in activities that provide more practice. The unit concludes with a forest art project that introduces antonyms and homonyms, along with a handy punctuation guide.

⁓ 92 ⁓

HOW TO WRITE A BOOK REPORT

When your child has read a particularly interesting book, encourage her jot down her thoughts about it. This outline will help her organize her thoughts so she can write a great report!

☞ **What You Need:**

Lined paper, pencil, book for report

☆ **Activity:**

Have your child follow this outline for her first report, but don't feel she needs to follow the format strictly. Encourage creative, from-the-heart writing, which is more interesting than simply answering the questions.

Book Report Outline

I. Read the book and make notes on important information.

II. Write a rough draft. Give each section (A–D below) its own paragraph.

    A. Give your reader important information about the book.

        1. Title

        2. Author's name

        3. Type of book

            a. Fiction

            b. Science fiction

            c. Nonfiction

            d. Biography

            e. Autobiography

        4. Number of pages

    B. Tell what the book is about. What happens?

    C. Describe your favorite part or character.

    D. Summarize your overall impression of the book as if you were talking with a friend.

III. Make corrections and write a second rough draft.

IV. Have a parent or teacher review your report. Make changes and write your final copy in cursive.

BOOK CLUB

The joy of reading is enhanced by sharing the experience with others. When friends gather to discuss books, it gives them the opportunity to think deeply about what they are reading and provides a friendly setting for sharing ideas. Listening to varied opinions broadens students' perspectives and helps them understand other people's points of view. Here are a few ideas for sponsoring a monthly book club.

☆ **Activity: Book Club**

Invite a few friends to read the same book each month. Then meet and discuss the following:

- The plot

- Favorite characters or events

- What the author could have done better

- How elements of the story relate to some aspect of the reader's life

More Ideas

Review the following suggestions with your child. Discuss how he wants to structure the club, then jot down ideas and decide on a plan of action.

1. Have each child read a favorite paragraph to the group.

2. Provide paper, colored pencils, or paints and have guests draw pictures of a scene in the book.

3. Do a craft project that relates to the book.

4. Choose a theme and ask each student write a poem or short story for next month's meeting. At that meeting, photocopy the pieces so that everyone has a copy. Let each child decorate a construction paper cover and staple it onto the stack of papers to form a booklet of the collected writings, which he can then take home.

5. Have members suggest a name for the Book Club. Decide the winner by secret ballot.

6. Schedule Book Club gatherings in students' homes, with the host providing snacks and drinks. Or meet in one location and assign one person to bring treats, rotating through the membership.

7. Invite an author or someone with an interesting travel experience or hobby to speak to the group. Have members write a thank-you letter that everyone signs.

8. Encourage students to read as many books as they can, then share their favorite ones with the group each month.

9. Invite each child to make a list of the books he has read and rate them with a five-star system—five being the best—by sticking gold stars (or drawing them) to the right of the titles.

Books !	
A Wrinkle in Time	☆ ☆ ☆
The Hobbit	☆ ☆ ☆ ☆ ☆
Redwall	☆ ☆ ☆ ☆
The History of Shipbuilding	☆ ☆ ☆
The Mystery of Skull Cave	☆ ☆
The Wizard of Oz	☆ ☆ ☆ ☆
Spiders Near and Far	☆ ☆ ☆
Folktales of Russia	☆ ☆ ☆
Black Beauty	☆ ☆ ☆ ☆
The Adventures of Tom Sawyer	☆ ☆ ☆
Podkayne of Mars	☆ ☆ ☆ ☆
Treasure Island	☆ ☆ ☆ ☆ ☆

94

How to Write a Report

on a Place

Ask your child to choose a city, state, or country that intrigues her and read about it in library books or on the internet. After collecting some facts about the place, have her use this outline as a guide to writing a report.

☞ What You Need:

Lined paper, pencil, research materials for report

☆ Activity:

Have your child use this outline to guide her research, note taking, arrangement of information, and writing of the report. Allow her to follow her interest while keeping suggested outline topics in mind. Answering the questions of one section may be enough for a first report, or she may wish to focus on a particular facet of the subject. The important thing is that she is reading, learning, and organizing her thoughts clearly in writing.

Geography Report Outline

I. Read from many sources, such as library books, magazines, and the internet. Make notes of important points.

II. Write a rough draft. Include information from some or all of these categories:

    A. Describe the place.

        1. What is its size?

        2. Where is it located?

        3. What is its climate?

        4. What does it look like?

    B. Summarize its early history.

        1. Who discovered it? Were there indigenous people living there?

        2. Why did people first go there?

    C. Describe the government.

        1. When or how did it become a city, state, or country?

        2. What form of government does it have?

        3. Who is the current leader?

    D. Recount important events that occurred in the area.

    E. Give examples of one or more things this area is know for (major exports, natural features, events, animals, agriculture, industry, etc.).

    F. Explain what you would like to see or do if you visited this place.

III. Make corrections and write a second rough draft.

IV. Have a parent or teacher review your report. Make changes and write your final copy in cursive.

95

How to Write a Biography

Learning about contemporary and historical figures will help expand your child's understanding of the world. This, in turn, may spark a spirit of inquiry leading to independent study beyond the original lesson. Instead of reporting on a famous person, he could interview and write about a family member, friend, or local business owner.

☞ **What You Need:**

Lined paper, pencil, biographical information (books, internet, or interview) on the life of a person

☆ **Activity:**

1. Invite your child to choose a person for his project. If it is someone he knows, he'll need to interview the subject and gather information for his report. For all others, he will read and collect facts from various materials. Make sure he has access to several sources so he can review contrasting points of view.

2. If he can't think of who to write about, suggest he choose someone from a field that interests him: author, scientist, explorer, musician, chef, actor, political leader, doctor, nurse, engineer, architect, artist, athlete, librarian, mechanic, teacher, inventor, etc.

3. Have your child use the following outline to guide his research and note taking, and to help him organize the final report.

Beethoven

Geography Report Outline

I. Read from many sources and gather notes for each section below.

II. Write a paragraph for A–E, below. This is your rough draft.

    A. Tell about the person's early life.

        1. Where and when was he or she born?

        2. Relate any interesting childhood experiences.

        3. What kind of education did the person have?

        4. Describe his or her character.

    B. Relate any life-changing experiences or relationships that influenced your subject's life.

    C. Describe the person's achievements.

    D. Summarize his or her later life. If you subject is still living, then adjust your answers accordingly.

        1. What work did he or she do?

        2. Where did he or she live?

        3. When did he or she die?

    E. Discuss what you learned from the individual's life.

III. Read your rough draft carefully and make corrections. Now read your rough draft aloud, slowly. Does each sentence convey new information flow smoothly, and make sense? Make additional corrections and write a second rough draft.

IV. Have a parent or teacher review your report. Make any indicated changes, and then write your final copy in cursive.

❧ 96 ❧

THE GRAMMAR RAINBOW

Make your child's early grammar experience enjoyable with these fun projects, which pair the seven rainbow colors with the seven main parts of speech (see guide on page 322).

- Nouns: red—name a person, place, thing, or idea (Jim, hut, dog, sadness)

- Pronouns: orange—substitute for a noun (I, me, you, us, we, them)

- Adjectives: yellow—describe a noun or pronoun (red, sharp, delicious)

- Verbs: green—show action or state of being (run, will eat, lived, am, was)

- Adverbs: blue (sky blue)—describe verbs, adjectives, adverbs (quickly, very, often, beautifully)

- Prepositions: indigo (dark blue)—establish a place (under, on, with, in)

- Conjunctions: violet—join words or groups of words (and, but, because)

☞ **What You Need:**

Scratch paper, construction paper in rainbow colors, pen or pencil, soft-lead colored pencils, seven envelopes, scissors, tape, bulletin board (or wall or large poster board), folder or basket

✄ **To Prepare: Grammar Rainbow**

1. Decide how large you want the rainbow to be.

2. Draw a rainbow template on scratch paper. Write the name of one color on each arc, in the order shown in the illustration on the next page.

3. Cut the rainbow template apart.

4. Use the pieces as guides to cut seven rainbow-colored arcs from colored construction paper.

5. Attach the rainbow arcs to a bulletin board, wall, or poster board.

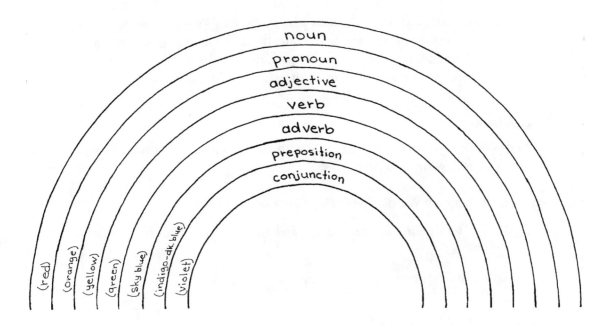

✄ **To Prepare: Word Slips**

Cut a dozen or more paper rectangles from each of the seven rainbow colors.

☆ **Activity 1:**

Introduce the Grammar Rainbow and say the colors with your child in order, from red to violet.

☆ **Activity 2:**

1. Discuss nouns with your child (see page 322). Have her name objects in your house. Explain that these words are nouns.

2. Write "noun" on the top of the largest (red) arc of the grammar rainbow. Encourage her to tell you more nouns, then write them down the right and left sides of the arc.

3. Ask her to write nouns on the prepared red slips of paper to make Word Slips. These may be the same or different from the ones on the rainbow.

4. Have her put the Word Slips into an envelope. Write "nouns" on the outside with red pencil or marker.

5. On another day, introduce the next part of speech. Write "pronoun" at the top of the second rainbow arc, add words from that category, and ask her to write pronouns on orange Word Slips. Continue in like fashion. Keep the envelopes with different parts of speech in a folder or basket.

☆ **Activity 3:**

Do this once you have done Activity 2 with all seven parts of speech. Have your child follow these steps:

1. Place a Rainbow Word Slip envelope on a table or carpet.

2. Take the Words Slips out, read them, and arrange them vertically beneath the envelope.

3. Take out another envelope and repeat.

Note: See the illustration on the next page.

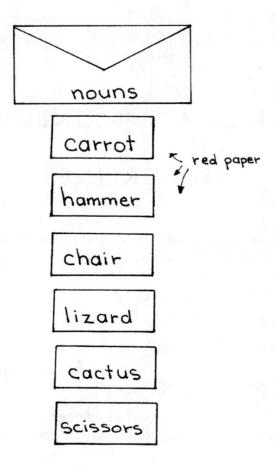

Variation:

1. Invite your child to build sentences with the Rainbow Word Slips.

2. Ask her to identify which part of speech describes each word.

3. Have her write the sentences on lined paper, using colored pencils that match each word's part-of-speech color.

✌ 97 ✌

Grammar Rainbow:

Underlines

Do this activity after the preceding Rainbow Grammar activities, when your child is comfortable finding words in each part of speech. At this point it would be helpful to acquire a grammar book for more advanced study.

☞ **What You Need:**

Lined paper, lead and colored pencils

✂ **To Prepare:**

With lead pencil, write simple sentences of your own composition or copied from books onto lined paper. See the next page for examples.

☆ **Activity:**

Demonstrate, then have your child mark the words in each sentence with a colored pencil corresponding to its grammar rainbow color to indicate its part of speech (see The Grammar Rainbow, page 396). Circle verbs in green. Draw a box around conjunctions in violet. Underline other words.

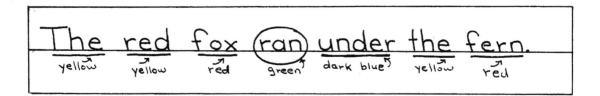

Examples:

Try these sentences, then make more of your own.

- The red fox ran under the fern.

- Peter and I ate a pickled purple beet!

- Annie is my dog.

- They are washing the car with soapy water.

- The toad sat on an old yellow leaf.

- Cucumbers, pumpkins, and watermelons grow on vines.

- You may make either raisin cookies or pecan bars.

- Tamara and Brad can swim fast.

- Can you teach me to sew? (In this sentence the verb *Can teach* is split by the subject (and pronoun) *you*. Circle both *Can* and *teach* with green pencil.)

- Is the water cold?

- Will Gary play the trumpet in the band?

- The parrot will peck the seeds.

- Fill the cup with hot chocolate. (In this sentence, the unwritten subject *you* (a pronoun) is understood. Write it in before the word *Fill* and underline it with orange when marking the sentence. Do the same with the next two sentences.)

- Set the three apples in the bowl.

- Kick the ball into the net.

- The earthworms wriggled and silently slid into the ground.

GRAMMAR GAME

Help reinforce the parts of speech while playing a game!

☞ **What You Need:**

Paper, pencils or pens, three-minute timer, two or more players

☆ **Activity:**

1. Have each player draw a chart with five rows and columns onto a sheet of paper.

2. Players choose four letters together, which they write in the boxes at left, and then print *noun, adj., verb,* and *adv.* in the spaces at the top, as shown in the illustration on the next page.

3. Start a timer, then each player fills in the chart as best she can. Adjectives must modify the chosen nouns; adverbs must modify the chosen verbs or adjectives. If a player fills the chart before the time is up, she may add more adjectives, verbs, or adverbs, but no nouns.

4. Points are counted after three minutes. One point is earned for each word.

	noun	adj.	verb	adv.
c	cat	white	purrs	softly
s	shoe	leather	shines	brightly
b	bucket	rusty	leaks	slowly
r	robin	hungry	ate	greedily

❧ 99 ❧

ADJECTIVE FLOWERS

Brighten up the house with colorful Adjective Flowers. This activity helps your child become familiar with adjectives and helps her understand that they modify nouns.

☞ **What You Need:**

Construction paper, colored markers, scissors, pictures of things (nouns)

☆ **Activity:**

Build one or more Adjective Flowers daily. Encourage your child to add petals when she thinks of new words and to consult a dictionary when she is unsure of the spelling.

1. Attach a picture of a thing, such as a lizard, beach, playground, lightning, octopus, apple pie, camel, ship, etc., on a bulletin board, wall, or large piece of paper. This is the center of the Adjective Flower.

2. Invite her to cut "petals" from construction paper.

3. With colored markers, have her write on each petal a word describing the image, and then attach the petals to the Adjective Flower picture.

Variation:

Instead of building the project on a wall, construct it on a sheet of paper. Your child can then make several pages of Adjective Flowers and bind them into a book.

⇝ 100 ⇝

ADJECTIVE CHART

Your child expands his vocabulary and strengthens his understanding of adjectives as he builds this week-long project.

☞ What You Need:

Construction paper, tape, colored markers, ruler, scissors

✂ To Prepare:

1. Cut five sheets of light-colored construction paper, so each one measures 8½- by 10-inches.

2. Draw four lines 2 inches apart down the sheets, as illustrated on page 307.

3. Cut a 2- by 8½-inch strip from the short end of a sixth sheet of construction paper. You will use this for the letter *z*.

4. Arrange the five prepared sheets short end to short end. Place the 2-inch strip (for *z*) next to the last paper on the right. Draw a horizontal line 1 inch down from the top edges of all the sheets.

5. Write the alphabet letters in the boxes at the top of the pages, as shown.

6. Tape the five sheets on a wall, as shown in the illustration. Attach the 2-inch strip, with the letter *z*, at the far right.

7. On construction paper, write a sentence or two that requires two adjectives. Try to choose two nouns that suggest contrasting descriptions. Draw a red line in place of the first adjective, and a green line in place of the second. Cut out the text and attach the strip above the chart.

Examples:

- The _____ witch lived in a remote castle. The _____ fairy lived in a silken treetop tent.

- The _____ cat eyed the _____ fish.

- The _____ dinosaur rushed to the _____ swamp.

- After the _____ sun set, the _____ moon rose.

- After walking over the _____ sand, Nancy and Franklin laughed as they jumped into the _____water.

- The _____ skyscraper loomed over the _____ cabin.

- The _____ basketball player glared at the _____ coach.

- The _____ owl was appointed mayor by the _____ wizard.

- The _____ horse peered inquisitively at the _____ mouse.

> The _____ witch lived in a remote castle. The _____ fairy lived in a silken treetop tent.

a	b	c	d	e	f	g	
able	big	caring	dull	educated	funny	gallant	
attractive	broad	creative	dutiful	elegant	fabulous	giant	
awful	bright	clumsy	delightful	excitable	ferocious	good	
	bad	calm	dingy	eager		gullible	
	bald						

☆ **Activity:**

1. Introduce the chart at the beginning of the week. Invite your child to read the sentence and imagine what kind of words would describe each noun.

2. Ask him to spend a few minutes writing adjectives onto the chart, placing each word under the letter with which it begins. Have him write the adjectives that apply to each noun in its matching color: red for the first, green for the second.

3. The object is not to have him try to fill the chart all at once, but to keep the lesson in mind by returning to it for a few minutes daily. Encourage him to add to the project anytime he thinks of another adjective that applies to one of the given nouns. His goal is to have adjectives in as many columns as possible by the end of the week. Invite him to use a dictionary or thesaurus to find additional words.

✌ 101 ✌

ADVERB GAME

This game emphasizes creative thinking while expanding vocabulary. It is best played with two or more people, but a single child can do it by racing against a three-minute or five-minute timer.

☞ **What You Need:**

Paper, pencil

☆ **Activity:**

1. Have each player write the letters of the alphabet vertically down the left side of a piece of paper.

2. Say a simple sentence that requires an adverb.

Examples:

- The plant grew _____.

- The man drove _____.

- The artist painted _____.

- The gymnast performed _____.

3. Set a timer for 3 or 5 minutes. Players write as many adverbs as they can think of next to the matching alphabet letters. The adverbs can be outlandish, but they should apply to the verb in some fashion.

4. If your child is racing alone against a timer, have her read you the finished list and comment on the various words. If playing in a group, have students compare their lists of words. One point is scored for each adverb shared by one or more players. Two points are scored for adverbs not written by another player. Use a dictionary to check spelling and find new words, if you wish.

The man drove ___.

a — annually
b — bumpily, briskly, bouncily
c — carelessly, creatively, circularly
d — drowsily, defensively, defiantly
e — effortlessly, effectively, eagerly
f
g

❧ 102 ❧

Alphabet Grammar Games

Quick! Pick a letter and name a noun, adjective, verb, or adverb. These two fast-paced games are great for reviewing parts of speech.

☞ **What You Need:**

    Cardstock, ruler, scissors, black or blue marker, paper and pencil (optional)

✄ **To Prepare:**

1. Cut a set of twenty-five 2¼- by 3½-inch cards from cardstock.

2. With black or blue marker, write the letters of the alphabet (except *x*) on the cards to make an Alphabet Card Deck.

☆ **Game 1: Name It!**

Play this for fun, not points. Setting a 3-, 5-, or 10-minute time limit can heighten excitement. Here's how to play:

1. Decide on a category: noun, verb, adjective, or adverb.

2. Shuffle the Alphabet Card Deck and place it face down.

3. A player takes the top card and quickly says a word that begins with that letter and fits the chosen grammar category. The solo player works quickly through the deck, saying a word for each letter he draws. Multiple players take turns drawing cards and saying a matching grammar word. Keep a dictionary handy to look up words.

Examples:

- **Nouns:** acorn, boot, corn, dove, elephant, fox, geranium, honey, Idaho, jack hammer, kite, library, mud, needle, olive, paper clip, quilt, redwood tree, swing, trampoline, undershirt, vase, willow, yeast, zebra

- **Verbs:** ambled, bucked, crawled, dove, edged, flew, growled, hopped, inched, jumped, kicked, lumbered, missed, neglected, ordered, pondered, questioned, raced, suggested, teased, understood, vacuumed, whistled, yawned, zoomed

- **Adjectives:** attractive, bright, cream-colored, decisive, educated, fabulous, generous, horrible, ignorant, juicy, knightly, loving, mossy, new, opulent, purple, quiet, regal, sleepy, tough, underground, valuable, western, yellow, zippy

- **Adverbs:** artfully, briskly, carelessly, drowsily, effortlessly, fast, gently, happily, innocently, joyfully, kindly, laughingly, moderately, noisily, often, purposefully, quickly, reverently, slowly, tasty, unquestioningly, very, wistfully, youthfully, zestfully

☆ Game 2: Grammar Categories

1. Decide on a category: noun, verb, adjective, or adverb.

2. Shuffle the deck and place it face down.

3. Decide on a short sentence that requires a word from your chosen category to complete.

4. A player takes the top card and quickly says the sentence, completing it using a word that begins with that letter and fits the chosen grammar category. The solo player works swiftly through the deck, saying a word for each letter he draws. Multiple players take turns drawing cards and saying a matching grammar word. Keep a dictionary handy to look up words.

Examples:

- **Nouns:**

    - I just read a book about _____. (goats, monkeys, ears, etc.)

    - I just saw a movie (or TV show) about _____.

    - My friend just told me about _____.

    - In my opinion, a _____ makes a fine pet.

- **Verbs:**

    - The king _____ that afternoon.

    - The whale _____.

    - The actor _____ on stage.

    - The robot didn't _____.

- **Adjectives:**

    - The _____ waitress took our order.

    - The _____ snake slithered under a rock.

    - The _____ toy sprang from the box.

    - Amy saw the _____ animal.

- **Adverbs:**

    - The clown was dressed _____.

    - The room was decorated _____.

    - The author wrote _____.

    - The bird sang _____.

    - Peter _____ painted the car last weekend.

Variation:

To score the game, set a time limit of 10 to 30 seconds per card. The player tries to name as many words as possible within the given time. For example, if the category is nouns and the letter is *s*, he might say, *sand, sand dollar, sled, spear, seed.* For each correct answer he gets one point. One point is detracted for each incorrect word, for example, *slid,* a verb; *silently,* an adverb; or *circle,* which starts with a *c.* Count the points after all the Alphabet Cards have been played.

❧ 103 ❧

Antonym and Homophone Forest

This ongoing project incorporates lots of movement. Whenever your child thinks of another set of antonyms or homophones, he adds them to the "forest" to help it grow. The activity brings his attention back to the subject repeatedly, which helps him learn the concept and expand his vocabulary.

☞ **What You Need:**

Foil, clay, popsicle sticks, construction paper, scissors, pen or colored marker; one or two old cookie sheets, trays, or a sheet of cardboard

✂ **To Prepare:**

1. Cover cookie sheets, trays, or a sheet of cardboard with foil. This is the base.

2. Prepare the ground for two separate forests by building two low mounds of clay on the base. One will become the Antonym Forest; the other will become the Homophone Forest (see illustration on page 317).

3. Cut green tree-shaped triangles from construction paper. These will be the Antonym Forest trees.

4. Cut scalloped, rounded tree shapes from autumn-leaf-colored construction paper: yellow, orange, brown, red. These will be the Homophone Forest trees.

☆ Activity 1: Build an Antonym Forest

1. Discuss antonyms—words that describe opposites—with your child. Examples: *black* and *white*, *up* and *down*, *right* and *left*, *good* and *bad*, *pain* and *pleasure*, *rough* and *smooth*, *wet* and *dry*, *tall* and *short*, *open* and *close*.

2. Have him write a pair of antonyms on two green tree triangles, one word per paper.

3. Glue them, back-to-back, onto the end of a popsicle stick. Press the stick into the clay base of the Antonym Forest.

4. Invite him to repeat the process with other word pairs. Set the Antonym Forest in a place where it can be reached easily and added to often. Remind him to build more word trees to make the forest grow.

☆ Activity 2: Build a Homophone Forest

1. Discuss homophones—words that sound alike but have different spellings and meanings—with your child (examples below).

2. Have him write a set of homophones on a piece of autumn-colored tree paper.

3. Glue the paper onto the end of a popsicle stick. Press the stick into the base of the Homophone Forest.

4. Invite him to continue building the forest with sets of homophones.

Examples:

- *bare* and *bear*
- *pair* and *pear* and *pare*
- *week* and *weak*
- *there* and *their* and *they're*
- *knight* and *night*
- *ate* and *eight*
- *cell* and *sell*

- *dear* and *deer*
- *horse* and *hoarse*
- *waist* and *waste*
- *peace* and *piece*
- *hole* and *whole*
- *berry* and *bury*
- *flower* and *flour*

- *hair* and *hare*
- *board* and *bored*
- *tale* and *tail*
- *male* and *mail*
- *ant* and *aunt*
- *die* and *dye*
- *doe* and *dough*

- *dew* and *do* and *due*
- *blue* and *blew*
- *heal* and *heel*
- *marry* and *merry*
- *pail* and *pale*
- *right* and *write*

- *knew* and *new*
- *sent* and *cent*
- *brake* and *break*
- *oar* and *or* and *ore*
- *pour* and *poor*
- *sew* and *so* and *sow*

- *beat* and *beet*
- *flew* and *flu*
- *loan* and *lone*
- *one* and *won*
- *sea* and *see*
- *ring* and *wring*

Antonym Forest

Homophone Forest

❧ 104 ❧

MY JOURNAL

Whether your child calls it a journal or diary, this final project offers a way to record her thoughts, observations, and experiences while developing a habit of writing daily. Encourage her to write for herself, explaining that this is her private journal, not school-work that you will review.

☞ **What You Need:**

Cardstock or other stiff paper, construction paper, lined writing paper (optional), colored pencils or pens, scissors, glue, hole punch, yarn or book binding rings

☆ **Activity:**

1. Invite your child to make a journal of her own, using the materials listed above or any others at hand.

2. Suggest she write in her journal often.

Examples:

Here are some ideas for writing topics:

- Jot down your daily activities

- In the evening, think about your day and record your thoughts about it. What went well? What could you do better next time?

- Make a To Do List for the following day.

- Recount funny or annoying things a pet does.

- Add pictures and descriptions of your favorite meals.

- Glue in pictures of special events such as birthday or holiday celebrations.

- Take time to observe something, then write a poem about it.

- Think about what you would like to accomplish in the next few months or year. Write a list of action steps you need to take to reach your goals.

- Choose a person that you admire and list the qualities that make them special. Describe how you can incorporate those ideals into your life.

- Think of one thing about yourself that you would like to improve. Jot down the steps you will take to do this.

- Make a list of your strong points. Write one per page and explain how you use them to help you. Give examples.

- Glue in ticket stubs from events. Add comments about your observations and experiences.

- When you finish reading a book, draw a picture of its cover. Write your impressions of it, along with new things you learned.

- Fill the pages with sketches. Doodle decorative borders.

- Do you have a bad habit? Find an action to replace it, then note your progress in the coming days.

- Choose a color and make that the theme of a page or two.

- Ask a relative to tell you a story from their childhood. Jot it down in your book.

- Think about what makes you happy and then write about it.

- Write about what makes you angry or sad. Think of ways to cope with those feelings or ways to change situations so those feelings don't arise. Add your ideas to your journal so you can refer to them again.

- Ponder how you can make someone else happy. List a few ways you can help them, then choose an action and do it!

- Make a list of your favorite songs.

- Write little stories with characters of your invention.

- When you hear a good joke or riddle, add it to your collection.

- Record the date when you accomplished something wonderful. Add lots of description so you'll remember it clearly in the future.

- Decide on a set of daily exercises and note which ones you do in the days ahead.

- Punch holes in the side of an interesting postcard and add it to your journal.

- When you find out odd, interesting facts, write them in your journal.

- Copy in a favorite recipe or compose your own meal ideas.

- Play with numbers. Invent your own mathematical problems and solve them for fun.

- When facing an important choice, make a list of pros and cons in your journal before making a decision.

- Measure your house and note the sizes of the rooms. Draw an illustration to go with your measurements.

- If you are musically inclined, hum a little tune and write it down.

- Use colored pencils or watercolors to paint a scene.

- Write to an imaginary friend or creature.

- Pick an alphabet letter. Write a short story or poem using many words beginning with that letter.

- Write your name vertically down the side of a page. Next to each letter, write words—that begin with that letter—that describe you.

- Make a list of your hopes and dreams. Your future self will delight in remembering what you were thinking at this time.

Variation:
Invite your child to make journals as gifts for friends.

CONCLUSION

I hope you spend many happy hours working through *Read, Write, & Spell.* The activities are offered as both a comprehensive guide and as suggestions to inspire you to create lessons of your own.

Along with the projects in this book, look for opportunities to reinforce language skills daily with conversation, reading, and writing. While doing dishes or riding in a car, for example, practice a few spelling words or recite a poem. Ask your child to write "to do" and shopping lists. And above all, provide lots of engaging reading material.

Looking back on our homeschooling experience, perhaps the most valuable piece of advice my husband and I can offer is this: Relax! Your child *will* learn to read and write. It is not the particular educational system you follow but the frequent practice of language skills that is important. When you can, find ways to connect lessons with a current favorite topic; this will heighten his interest in the material. And give him time to think, to daydream, to explore the world at his own pace, for that is when he may discover passions that will be key to his future.

Young children have little sense time but live fully in the moment. While you are focused on a project's result, your child is absorbed in the process of doing it. When our son, Christopher, was little, he would mix together several colors of finger paint until he had muddy-colored glop. Meanwhile, his sister, Angela, made pretty, colorful patterns. At the end of the day, when the art was dry, his sister's pictures were more pleasing to view. It wasn't until Christopher was an adult that he explained that it was the process of swirling the paint together that interested him most. He was fascinated by the white trails his fingers made as he dragged them through the paint; as he concentrated on them, he felt as though he were being drawn into a three-dimensional world. Wow! All we adults saw was muck.

I wish you all the best with your schooling adventure!

Talita Paolini

PARTS OF SPEECH

Here is a quick review of the fundamental components of grammar. Teach your child these basics so he will understand how the language is constructed. For more detailed advice, either search online or look in any grammar book.

- **Nouns** name something, such as a person, animal, place, thing, or idea: *tree, violin, whale, house, chair, dinner, music, pencil, noise, friend, happiness.* A **proper noun** names a specific person, place, or thing, such as *Mary, James, Grandma Julia, Honda, Peru, Santa Fe,* or *Reed College.*

- **Pronouns** are words that substitute for nouns. **Personal pronouns** refer to people or things: *I, me, you, he, him, she, her, it, we, us, you, they, them.* Some other pronouns are *who, whom, whoever, whomever, what, which, whose, another, everything, most, somebody, that, what, which, who, whom, whoever, whomever,* and *whose.* The words *this, that, these,* and *those* function as pronouns when used to replace the name of something: Tricia likes the coat. Tricia likes *that.* **Possessive pronouns** show ownership: *mine, your, his, hers, its, ours, yours, theirs, my, your, his, her, our, your, their.*

- **Adjectives** modify nouns or pronouns. They tell what kind, which one, how many, and whose. Examples: *red* ball, *soft yellow* dress, *Anita's delicate* hands, *spiny* cactus, Fred looked *happy. This, that, these,* and *those* sometimes act as adjectives: *This* ball. *That* cactus. The **Articles** *a, an,* and *the* are also adjectives.

- **Verbs** are words or groups of words that describe an action or state of being. Examples: *run, runs, ran, has run, will run, did run, will be running, sleep, sing, think, walked, drove, am, was, were, are, is, feel, taste.*

- **Adverbs** modify verbs, adjectives, other adverbs, or the whole sentence by telling how, when, where, how often, and to what extent: ran *quickly, slowly* walked, looked *everywhere,* sang *very sweetly, soon* decided, *never* hungry, sang *later, not* sleepy, *very* young child.

- **Prepositions** establish a relationship between a noun or pronoun and some other word in the sentence. Some common prepositions are *after, under, around, between, above, in, over, on, to, during, since, through, till, with, up, until, within, in front of, because of,* and *in addition to.*

- **Conjunctions** are words that join words and groups of words. Here are some common conjunctions: *and, but, for, nor, or, so, yet, although, because, until, either . . . or, neither . . . nor.*

PUNCTUATION GUIDE

Punctuation marks clarify the meanings of sentences and—like traffic signs—tell readers when to pause and stop. They also alert readers to dramatic parts, questions, lists, and direct quotes. Review the rules of punctuation with your child and encourage her to incorporate the marks in her writing. Refer to a grammar book for a more thorough discussion of the subject.

Three Punctuation Marks that Say Stop!

<u>Period</u>:
A period means stop and is placed at the end of most sentences. It is also used with abbreviations.

- Used at the end of a sentence.

  ➝ The clown has a red balloon.

- Used after an abbreviation.

  ➝ Mr., Mrs., Dr., Nov., etc., in., min.

<u>Question Mark</u>:
A question mark is placed at the end of a sentence or phrase to indicate a direct question.

    ➝ Did you find the chocolate bars?

    ➝ "Who washed the dog?" she asked.

    ➝ Mom asked, "Who washed the dog?"

<u>Exclamation Mark:</u>
While it is fine to practice using the exclamation mark in writing exercises, remember that it denotes *strong* feelings, such as fear, surprise, determination, anger, joy, awe, or shock. Good writers express their ideas with well-chosen words and use the exclamation mark sparingly.

- Used at the end of sentences to show strong emotion.

  → The dog ate my hamburger!

- Used to show strong emotion after an interjection.

  → Wow! That throw was phenomenal.

Note: For interjections of a milder nature, use a comma instead of an exclamation mark.

> → Well, I didn't know what to think.

> → My goodness, you surprised me.

Eight Rules for Commas

Commas help clarify sentences by telling readers where to pause. Sometimes the placement or omission of a comma can change the meaning of a sentence or cause confusion, as in these examples:

> → After the horse bucked, Susan Marie ran for help.

> After the horse bucked Susan, Marie ran for help.

> → After the swimmer ate the crowd watched him leave the restaurant.

> After the swimmer ate, the crowd watched him leave the restaurant.

These rules will help you use commas correctly:

Comma Rule #1: Items in a Series
Use to separate items in a list.

→ The fireworks were blue, yellow, white, and red.

→ Season the stew with parsley, rosemary, and thyme.

→ Jerry, Sarah, and Martin went to the movies.

Comma Rule #2: To Set Off Names
When addressing a person: use a comma after a name at the beginning of a sentence, before a name at the end of a sentence, and around a name in the middle of a sentence.

→ Mary, did you dust the piano?

→ On second thought, Jan, you may have another half hour to read before bed.

→ The present was wonderful, Tom.

Comma Rule #3: Before Conjunctions
Use a comma before the words *and, but, or, yet,* and *for* when they join two phrases with two subjects.

→ The pudding was good, but the cake was better.

→ Sandra will ride her bike, and Mike will take the bus.

→ It was a great party, yet I wish Mary could have attended.

→ Micah went to town, and he visited the museum.

Note: Do not put a comma after a conjunction that joins two phases that share the original subject without restating it:

→ Micah went to town and visited the museum.

Comma Rule #4: After Phrases that Need a Pause
Use a comma after a word or phrase at the beginning of a sentence that needs a pause.

→ Yes, your paper looks good.

→ Later, she picked the yellow rose.

→ In case of fire, go to the exit.

→ When driving at night, be sure to take a flashlight.

→ Setting up the tent, he discovered a stake was missing.

Note: Commas are not usually used after the words *but, and,* and, *yet* at the beginning of a sentence. Do not use a comma after words or short phrases at the beginning of sentences if it would interrupt the flow with an unnecessary pause.

→ Now Ann is really a nice person, if you give her a chance.

→ Therefore we painted the fence quickly.

→ But then we discovered the treasure.

→ And Jerry commented on the new racing tires.

Comma Rule #5: Set Apart Non-Essential Phrases
Use commas to set apart expressions and phrases that are not essential to, or that interrupt the flow of, a sentence.

→ Nancy, who lives next door, will be your teacher.

→ The computer works quicker, I think, with the new system.

→ After singing in the choir, Sam went home.

→ Watching that movie, in my opinion, is a waste of time.

→ I think fresh garden vegetables, aside from Brussels sprouts, are delicious.

<u>Comma Rule #6</u>: Before or After Quotation Marks
Use commas to indicate a pause before or after direct speech set off by quotation marks.

→ "The hole could be deeper," said Joshua, "but I think it will do."

→ The zoo keeper remarked, "The monkeys seem lively today."

→ "Come to the pool with me," Carrie called.

<u>Comma Rule #7</u>: In Dates, Addresses, and Numbers
Use commas in dates, addresses, and to divide large numbers.

→ Her birthday is April 6, 2010.

→ Frances Smith, 23 Lark Street, Avondale, CA 90000

→ All-Weather Construction Company bought 129,620 nails.

<u>Comma Rule #8</u>: To Separate Adjectives
Use commas to separate adjectives that describe a noun in a similar way and that could be linked by the word *and*. Do not add commas between words that describe a noun in different ways.

→ The pungent, fragrant spices roasted in the pan.

→ A bright yellow rose decorated the table.

→ The sparkling two thousand-bead necklace sold for three million dollars.

→ The red, blue, and yellow candies tempted him.

→ Henry didn't want the ugly, broken bike.

→ Sarah spilled five cups of fancy toasted nuts.

Colons, Semicolons, and Quotation Marks

Colons:
A colon signals the reader that a list (providing additional details or explanation) or quotation follows.

- Use a colon after a complete statement to introduce a list.

  → The orchard contains six varieties of trees: peach, pear, nectarine, walnut, pecan, and almond.

  → Uncle James likes to do several things at the beach: surf, meet with friends, explore the tide pools, and photograph the waves.

- Use a colon to introduce a formal quote.

  → Mark Twain ends his short story, "Tom Quartz," with these words: "The affection and the pride that lit up Baker's face when he delivered this tribute to the firmness of his humble friend of other days will always be a vivid memory with me."

- A colon follows the salutation in a formal letter. It also divides hours and minutes, and the chapter and verse of Bible scripture.

  → Dear Mr. Campbell:

  → The concert starts at 7:30 a.m. sharp.

  → I read Genesis 9:16 last evening.

Semicolons:
Semicolons are like very strong commas. They typically join two sentences that could stand alone but are better linked; they show that the sentences are closely related. Semicolons also work as super-commas to divide lists containing a confusion of commas.

- Use semicolons to link like sentences.

  → Five apples are red; six are green.

  → She spoke three languages; her father taught her two of them.

  → The ice cream was melting; it oozed onto the table and dripped on the floor.

- Use semicolons to separate items in a series that contain commas.

  → Celia provided cat, dog, and fish stickers; striped, dotted, and starred pencils; and yellow, pink, green, and blue balloons for party favors.

  → The mouse nibbled cheese, crackers, and apples; scratched out paths and runways; and gnawed the edges of table legs, chairs, and cupboards.

Quotation Marks:

To quote means to repeat the exact words of a person. We use quotation marks to bracket those words. When writing dialogue, begin a new paragraph each time a different person speaks, even if it is only one sentence.

- Use quotation marks around the exact words of a speaker.

  → Rudy said, "Roll up the rug."

  → "Catch the rooster!" Aunt Ellen yelled.

  → Mr. Fisher asked, "Where shall I put the harp?"

  → "When we were your age," said Kelly, "we climbed that tree."

  → Milla told me that she likes strawberries and that she "ate them all up!"

- Place quotation marks around the titles of short works such as magazine articles, short stories, poems, book chapters, and songs.

  → We all sang "Happy Birthday" to Steven.

  → "The Kitten at Play," by William Wordsworth, is a delightful poem for children.

Three Dashes

Dashes come in three lengths: the shortest is called the hyphen, the one of middle length is called the en-dash, and the longest is the em-dash.

Hyphen:
The hyphen is used to link words together, usually two adjectives modifying a noun. A hyphen is required when the adjectives would not make sense if used alone.

- Used to link words.
  - → The sky-blue sapphire ring gleamed on her finger.
  - → The five-year-old donkey pulled the cart.
  - → The algae-covered pond was green.
  - → Orange-skinned pumpkins are ripe.
  - → Foil-wrapped chocolates are pretty.
  - → First-, second-, and third-grade girls sang.
  - → The log is one-half meter long.
- Use between numbers from twenty-one to ninety-nine.
- Use with some prefixes, especially those before a capitalized word.
  - → He visited the sub-Sahara desert.
  - → His ex-wife's name is Delores.
  - → Let's go to Oregon in mid-June.
  - → The all-American player won a medal.
  - → The all-pervasive smell filled the room.
  - → She was born in the mid-1980s.

<u>En-Dash:</u>

Slightly longer than a hyphen, the en-dash joins groups of words, years, or numbers.

→ The 40–50 pound squash was striped green and yellow.

→ The 1960–1970 fashions included bell-bottom pants and long hair.

→ The plane follows the Seattle–Spokane–Salt Lake City route.

→ The Barbie–Ken dolls are holiday favorites.

→ Bake the bread for 45–50 minutes.

<u>Em-Dash:</u>

This longest of the dashes is commonly called a *dash*. It's name comes from the fact that it is as wide as a capital *M*. The em-dash is used to denote a remark or thought outside of a sentence's general flow. It can take the place of commas, parentheses, or colons to add emphasis or clarity.

→ Charlotte makes the most beautiful dolls—which she sells at a local gift shop—with braided hair and button eyes.

→ Jacob—a remarkable man—told us the history of his homeland, the Netherlands.

→ Charlie built a model-train track in his yard—an amazing creation of hills, trees, and miniature houses.

→ After counting the cups—all sixteen of them—Alyssa discovered that she was missing three.

Resource Index

A collection of resources you'll find in this book and online.

In This Book

Word Lists:

Instructions:

Miscellaneous:

- Alphabet Rhyme: Lesson 4, page 50
- Alphabet Picture Ideas: Lesson 6, page 56–58
- Printed Writing Samples: Lesson 13, page 82
- Cursive Writing Samples: Lesson 63, pages 222, 224
- Rules for Capitalization: Lesson 63, pages 224, 225
- Parts of Speech: pages 322, 323
- Punctuation Guide: pages 324–332

Free Online Downloadable Content

Visit paolinimethod.com/downloads to access the materials below.

Illustrations:

- Alphabet Pictures–large Alphabet Pictures–small
- Short Vowel Word Pictures–large
- Short Vowel Word Pictures–small
- Partner Word Pictures

Writing Paper:

- Large paper: ⅞-inch-rule lined writing paper
- Small paper: ⅝-inch-rule lined writing paper

Word Lists:

- Short Vowel Words
- Long Vowel Partner Words

Acknowledgments

Many wonderful people have influenced my life. Had any one of them been missing, I doubt that this book would exist. When I think of them, I feel great fondness and these memories come to mind:

My mother:
> *Myself as a young child walking hand-in-hand with my mother as she points out soft green moss, shiny yellow buttercups, and dainty mushroom fairy-rings.*

My teacher:
> *Myself as a student of the vibrant eighty-year-old Dr. Elisabeth Caspari, watching her effortlessly touch her toes and then raise her fingers to the sky while teaching a classroom of bright-eyed students. Quiet sessions with her as she shared the knowledge and experience from her long association with Maria Montessori.*

My family:
> *Myself as a wife and the mother of two beautiful children, facing—together with my husband—the daunting task of raising and educating them.*
>
> *Myself after three decades of marriage, reflecting on my children (now adults), who helped me understand the nature of childhood, and for whom I developed and adapted many of these lessons.*

Thanks to my family for their loving support of this project. Specifically, I'm grateful to my son, Christopher, for drawing the more difficult pictures; my daughter, Angela, for her encouragement and editing prowess; and my husband, Kenneth, for his help formatting the illustrations and text.

A huge thank you to my assistant, Immanuela Meijer, whose keen intellect and sharp red pencil helped wrangle this manuscript into shape. Her help scanning and formatting the illustrations, getting all the downloadable content online, and figuring out how to get the manuscript to the printer is greatly appreciated. And when I got stuck on a few illustrations, she came to my rescue in that department too!

Finally, my gratitude goes to Tara Mayberry, who designed the beautiful cover.

Talita Paolini
Livingston, Montana, USA
December, 2018

Teach with confidence and spark your child's joy of learning with these Paolini Method books!

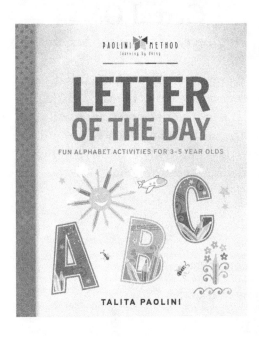

LETTER
of the Day
Fun Alphabet Activities
for 3–5 year olds

Tap into your child's curiosity with activities that introduce the alphabet through crafts and playful exploration of the environment. With 104 lessons to choose from, it's easy to find ones that spark excitement. Just pick a letter, do the project, and soon your little one will be pointing out letters everywhere and scribbling them for fun!

- Learn letter sounds and shapes
- Begin to write the alphabet
- Improve coordination
- Build concentration skills
- Discover how to find answers to questions
- Become more aware of their surroundings

Letter of the Day
Talita Paolini
228 pages, softcover
ISBN: 9780966621365

Order from paolinimethod.com or any bookstore.

Play & Learn with Cereal O's
Language, Math, and Science

Play & Learn with Cereal O's makes it easy to teach the basics of math, reading, writing, and scientific observation. All you need are cereal O's and a few household items. This collection of simple, effective activities makes learning fun!

- Improve coordination and develop concentration
- Learn letter sounds and discover how to read
- Write words and sentences
- Name and write the numbers
- Count and associate numbers with amounts
- Experience basic addition, subtraction, multiplication, and division
- Build, draw, and identify geometric figures
- Learn about the solar system
- Build a balance scale, measure small items, chart data, and more!

Play & Learn with Cereal O's
Talita Paolini
112 pages, softcover
ISBN: 9780966621372   Order from paolinimethod.com or any bookstore.

❧ STAY IN TOUCH ❧

I wrote these lessons to share what I've learned as a teacher and parent, and with hope that my suggestions will make your teaching adventure easier. As you watch your child's language skills bloom, consider sharing your stories and photos on social media—using #PaoliniMethod—to inspire others with your projects.

Facebook: facebook.com/paolinimethod

Twitter: twitter.com/paolinimethod

Instagram: instagram.com/paolinimethod

Pinterest: pinterest/paolinimethod

And come visit my website, PaoliniMethod.com, where you'll discover more fun educational activities!

Talita

CPSIA information can be obtained
at www.ICGtesting.com
Printed in the USA
LVHW051536010920
664770LV00006B/267